SAFETY, CULTURE AND RISK

The Organisational Causes of Disasters

Disclaimer

No person should rely on the contents of this publication without first obtaining advice from a qualified professional person. This publication is sold on the terms and understanding that (1) the authors, consultants and editors are not responsible for the results of any actions taken on the basis of information in this publication, nor for any error in or omission from this publication; and (2) the publisher is not engaged in rendering legal, accounting, professional or other advice or services. The publisher, and the authors, consultants and editors, expressly disclaim all and any liability and responsibility to any person, whether a purchaser or reader of this publication or not, in respect of anything, and of the consequences of anything, done or omitted to be done by any such person in reliance, whether wholly or partially, upon the whole or any part of the contents of this publication. Without limiting the generality of the above, no author, consultant or editor shall have any responsibility for any act or omission of any other author, consultant or editor.

SAFETY, CULTURE AND RISK

The Organisational Causes of Disasters

ANDREW HOPKINS

CCH AUSTRALIA LIMITED

GPO Box 4072, Sydney, NSW 2001

Head Office North Ryde   Phone: (02) 9857 1300   Fax: (02) 9857 1600

Customer Support   Phone: 1300 300 224   Fax: 1300 306 224

www.cch.com.au

Book Code: 3905A

About CCH Australia Limited

CCH Australia Limited is part of a leading global organisation publishing in many countries.

CCH publications cover a wide variety of topic areas, including tax, accounting, finance, superannuation, company law, contract law, conveyancing, torts, occupational health and safety, human resources and training.

CCH has published two other books by Andrew Hopkins, *Lessons from Longford: The Esso Gas Plant Explosion* and *Lessons from Longford: the Trial*.

More information about these, and about other products, can be found on the CCH website at *www.cch.com.au*.

National Library of Australia Cataloguing-in-Publication Data

Hopkins, Andrew, 1945 —
Safety, Culture and Risk: the organisational causes of disasters.

1st ed.
Includes index
ISBN 1 921022 25 6

1. Australia. Royal Australian Air Force — Safety measures.
2. Corporate culture — Australia. 3. Risk assessment.
4. Disasters — Case studies. 5. Railroad accidents — New South Wales — Glenbrook.
I. CCH Australia Limited. II. Title.

363.1

Printed in Australia by McPherson's Printing Group

ISBN 1 921022 25 6

The publisher has made every effort to identify and contact the copyright holder of the image used on the jacket. The copyright holder is invited to contact the publisher with proof of copyright.

Foreword

An early meeting with Andrew Hopkins was at a conference on workplace safety in Sweden four years ago. There we heard a recently appointed director of safety in a large British company assert that safety management was not rocket science. He was right, of course, but perhaps not in the way he intended. The challenge of rocket science pales in comparison to the complexities of safety management. There are only so many ways of launching and recovering a spacecraft, but there are not enough trees in the rainforest upon which to write safety procedures that would guarantee complete freedom from harm in even a relatively simple activity. In short, managing safety is by far the most difficult task in any hazardous endeavour.

The complexities arise not only from the myriad ways in which people, assets and the environment can be damaged, but also because the focus of safety management has become increasingly more diffuse. For example, in the early days of commercial aviation, safety threats came mainly from technical or mechanical failures. But, as the technology advanced and aircraft became more reliable, human performance problems came into increasingly greater prominence. Estimates of human error as a causal factor increased from 20% to 30% in the 1960s, to 80% to 90% in the 1990s. However, a number of sentinel events in various domains — Tenerife, Mt Erebus, Chernobyl, Zeebrugge, King's Cross, Clapham, to name but a few — soon made it clear that those people at the "sharp end" in direct contact with each system were not so much the instigators of bad events as the inheritors of an "accident in waiting" that had, in some cases, been lying dormant within the system for many years.

Much as it was (and still is) managerially and legally convenient to blame those on the front line, it was gradually becoming apparent that accidents in well-defended systems arose from a concatenation of many different factors arising from all levels of the organisation. The defining feature of such an "organisational accident" was that these latent systemic conditions, in combination with local triggers, opened up a brief window of accident opportunity through the system's barriers, controls and safeguards, allowing the local hazards to come into damaging contact with people or assets.

These "defences in depth" are usually many and varied: some are physical barriers, others are engineered safety features, and others comprise administrative controls, procedures, briefings and personal safety equipment. An organisational accident can arise only when all or most of these defences are breached. In complex systems, this involves a large measure of bad luck. But there is often something else at work — something that reaches all parts of the system for good or ill. And this brings me to the topic of this book, *safety culture*.

Safety culture is a term that has been widely used over the past few years. Even though few people can agree on exactly what it means, it has become an increasing matter of concern. We are in desperate need of guidance, and this is what this book offers.

Andrew Hopkins is a consummate storyteller as well as being an internationally known expert on the breakdown of hazardous socio-technical systems. I believe that only stories such as those told here can capture the subtle influences of organisational culture and embrace the complex interactions between causes and conditions. This book is essential reading for safety practitioners, academics and all students of the safety sciences.

James Reason
Author, *Managing the Risks of Organisational Accidents*

Professor James Reason is Emeritus Professor of Psychology at The University of Manchester

CCH wishes to thank the following team members who contributed to this publication

Editor: Karen Enkelaar, Dowrite

Production editors: Felicia Gardner, Deb Robertson

Indexers: Beverley Kirkby, Mark Southwell

Marketing: Catherine Bunt, Robert Sawyer

Cover design: Danielle Kojic, Design Animals

Product development: Penny Martin

Publisher: Nathan Moyes

Contents

Introduction

A recent best seller is entitled *Eats, Shoots and Leaves* (Truss, 2003). Punctuated in this way, the title refers to three separate activities: eating, shooting and leaving. If the comma is removed, the meaning of the title changes totally. It refers to the single activity of eating the shoots and leaves of plants. Such is the difference a comma can make!

Should this book *Safety, Culture and Risk* have a comma in its title? Without the comma, the book would be about two ideas: "safety culture" and "risk". With the comma, however, safety culture becomes two separate ideas: "safety" and "culture".

This book is indeed about the idea of safety culture. But it is also about the more general relationship between culture and safety. Both meanings are therefore intended. I include the comma to signal the greater scope of this work.

Let me be clearer about the difference. Every organisation has a culture and that culture can be expected to impact on safety. Understanding how this happens will provide insights into ways organisational cultures can be modified to give a higher priority to safety. The concept of safety culture does not fully encompass the complex relationship between the culture of an organisation and its safety performance. This is one of its limitations.

A second limitation is that the meaning of safety culture is ambiguous. According to one usage, all organisations have a safety culture of some sort, which might be either positive or negative, strong or weak. According to another usage, only an organisation which has an overriding commitment to safety can be said to have a safety culture. On this latter view, "safety culture" can be used interchangeably with "culture of safety", and that is how I use the term in this book.

The book is divided into four parts. Part A deals initially with the meaning of culture and its relationship to safety. I shall argue that the concept of organisational culture is widely understood as the *mindset* of its *individuals*, but that it is better seen as the *collective practices* of an *organisation*. I conclude that efforts to change cultures should be focused not on changing individual values but on changing organisational practices.

This argument is followed by a discussion of safety culture and two related ideas — organisational mindfulness, and risk-awareness. The latter two are both essentially cultural phenomena and both are nowadays advocated as ways of enhancing safety. I shall show that these two ideas overlap to a considerable extent with the concept of safety culture. They are different ways of talking about the same cultural phenomena, with very similar implications for achieving safe operation. They can be defeated, however, by cultures of risk-denial, as will also be discussed in this part.

Parts B and C are case studies of how organisational cultures can undermine health and safety. Part B deals with a train crash near Sydney in 1999 which killed seven people — the Glenbrook train crash. This is the longest section of the book and provides a detailed analysis of the accident. There have been two rail disasters causing major losses of life in New South Wales, Australia in recent years and three in the United Kingdom, and the analysis here is relevant to them all.[1] Four main constellations of practices and hence four cultural themes are identified as contributing to the accident: a culture of rules, a culture of "silos",[2] a culture of on time running, and a risk-blind, even risk-denying culture.

Part C, the second case, examines how the health of more than 400 maintenance workers at Amberley Air Force base near Brisbane was ruined by exposure to toxic chemicals over a 20-year period. Among the Air Force values which contributed to this outcome were: the priority of air safety over ground safety, the "can do" attitude, and the priority given to machines over people. The case has considerable relevance for many airlines where similar values are in evidence.

These two cases are interesting in that they are also examples of organisations doing certain things very well. In the case of the railways, the attention paid to running on time was astonishing, while in the case of the Air Force, the attention paid to air safety was exemplary. These successes are analysed in cultural terms in order to draw lessons about what is needed to create a culture of safety.

Sceptics might argue that a cultural approach to safety is just the latest fashion and that the various concepts mentioned above — safety culture, organisational mindfulness and risk-awareness — are part of the fashion parade. If the insights yielded by the cultural approach are not in the end applied, the sceptics will be right in one sense; namely, that all this is theorising, which makes no practical difference. But there is another sense in which the cultural approach is immune to the critics. The claim which I hope to demonstrate, especially in Parts B and C, is that the culture of an organisation determines its safety performance. Readers may decide for themselves whether or not they are convinced by this argument.

The earlier parts of this book deal with risk-awareness without locating it in a broader discussion on risk and risk management. Part D consists of two discrete chapters which aim to provide this broader context.

---

1   Glenbrook and Waterfall in New South Wales, Australia, and Southall, Ladbroke Grove and Hatfield in England.

2   Grain silos in rural areas are isolated from one another. The metaphor refers to the way parts of an organisation can be similarly disconnected.

There is mounting evidence that, within the sequence of hazard identification, risk assessment and risk control, risk assessment has been given far too much prominence and that the more important issues are identifying hazards and putting in place effective controls.

For example, consider the following event recounted to me by the manager of an outback production facility. A works vehicle, travelling on a road near the facility, had hit a pothole and swerved to the other side of the road before the driver recovered control. The facility was in a remote location and the chances of hitting an oncoming car were very slight. But if there had been a collision, it might have resulted in a fatality.

How was the risk to be assessed? The manager was required to decide on a risk score before deciding on what control measures were appropriate, but he was stuck because he was not sure how to rate this risk. This was a situation in which it made sense to bypass the risk assessment stage altogether. A hazard had been identified and the obvious risk control measure was to fill the pothole. Attempting to assess the risk was a potentially fatal distraction.

Sometimes the risk assessment stage is understood to require quantitative estimates of the risk. The first chapter in Part D deals with the perils of quantitative risk assessment and the associated concept of acceptable risk. It shows that quantitative estimates are highly questionable, and that the idea of an acceptable level of risk is not only morally and practically flawed but is, in principle, inconsistent with the legal requirement that risks be reduced so far as is reasonably practicable. The chapter argues that in so far as risk assessment is actually necessary, qualitative assessments by professionally competent people will normally be sufficient. Quantitative risk assessment is a powerful idea with a tendency to carry all before it. Risk-awareness, on the other hand is an elusive concept, easily swamped. The ultimate argument of this chapter is that organisations striving to be risk-aware need to be wary of quantitative risk assessment. I am indebted to Mark Tweeddale for his detailed comments on this chapter.

The second chapter in Part D engages with the intriguing idea that risk is now such an important issue that we can sensibly speak of the development of a new kind of society, "risk society". The chapter argues that the proponents of the risk society theory are confused and that, in so far as they are arguing that modern society faces unprecedented levels of risk, they are wrong. In fact, we live in a society in which risks are more controllable than ever; hence, the increasing demand that they *be* controlled. The chapter provides some insight into the increasing pressure which organisations are under to construct cultures of safety.

The four parts of this book are relatively self-contained. Not everyone will be interested in quantitative risk assessment or in the debate about "risk society". Some will be more interested in the story of the Glenbrook rail crash or the Air Force case study than in the more conceptual discussion of Part A. If you get most out of reading accounts of disasters, these two cases may be a good place to start. Finally, because of this segmented structure, there is no overall conclusion. I trust you will find something here of interest!

Andrew Hopkins
Canberra
(Andrew.Hopkins@anu.edu.au)
September 2004

part A

Chapter 1
Safety culture, collective mindfulness and risk-awareness

Introduction

Safety culture is one of a number of ideas currently seen as offering organisations a way to achieve higher standards of safety. A second concept which seems to spark interest whenever it is mentioned is collective mindfulness, advocated by Karl Weick and his associates (Weick and Sutcliffe, 2001). Risk-awareness is a third, related concept. These ideas all involve a cultural approach to safety and, as I shall show, are essentially alternative ways of talking about the same cultural phenomena.

It is crucial to have a clear idea of the concept of culture before embarking on any analysis of the cultural approaches to safety. This chapter therefore contains an extended discussion of the topic and also of the vital role that leadership plays in creating cultures. It begins, though, with an account of why the cultural approach is now so prominent.

Why the cultural approach?

The attention now being paid to the cultural approach to safety stems in part from a recognition of the limitations of safety management systems as a means of achieving safety. For the last couple of decades, safety professionals, regulators and others have been arguing that safety is not simply a matter of compliance with externally imposed regulations. Instead, organisations need to manage safety proactively in the same way that they manage their other activities. They need, in short, to develop safety management systems.

Experience with safety management systems suggests, however, that they are not infallible. Major accidents are frequently traced to failures in safety management systems (Appleton, 2001), and investigations sometimes reveal that safety management systems are little more than sets of manuals occupying metres of shelf space and bearing little relation to what goes on in the workplace. They are *virtual* safety management systems, existing in theory but not in practice (VWA, 2001).

The Royal Commission of Inquiry into the Esso's gas plant explosion near Melbourne in 1998 came close to describing the safety management system at the site as virtual. Esso was using a system developed by the parent company

Exxon, known as OIMS (Operations Integrity Management System). Here is what the Commission had to say about the system:

> "OIMS, together with all the supporting manuals, comprised a complex management system. It was repetitive, circular, and contained unnecessary cross-referencing. Much of its language was impenetrable. These characteristics made the system difficult to comprehend by management and by operations personnel.
>
> The Commission gained the distinct impression that there was a tendency for the administration of OIMS to take on a life of its own, divorced from operations in the field. Indeed it seemed that in some respects, concentration upon the development and maintenance of the system diverted attention from what was actually happening in the practical functioning of the plants at Longford (Dawson and Brooks, 1999:13.39-13.40)."

It would be hard to imagine a more devastating critique of a safety management system.

Evidence of another sort comes from a study carried out some years ago of safety management systems in South African mines (Eisner and Leger, 1988). Safety management at these mines had been assessed using the International Safety Rating System (the five star system). The study sought to correlate the number of stars achieved by these mines with their fatality and reportable injury rates. It found no correlation. In other words, companies which had perfected their systems and whose achievement had been recognised with a five star rating were no safer than companies whose safety management systems were judged to be inferior. This is a sobering finding, reinforcing the view that safety cannot be assured simply by introducing a safety management system.

There is plenty of anecdotal evidence as well. An Australian company which consistently achieved five star ratings for years, became aware of a disturbing number of "near misses". One particular near miss brought matters to head: its electrical isolation procedures failed and an electrician began work on a live piece of high-voltage equipment. Evidently its five star system was not good enough (see also Shaw and Blewitt, 2000:460).

None of this is to suggest that safety management systems are unnecessary. It is simply that something else is needed to bring them to life, to make them work — and that something is an appropriate organisational culture.

Here is how one of the foremost writers in this area, Jim Reason, puts it in an article entitled "Beyond the limitations of safety systems":

"[There is a] widely spread misconception ... that somehow systems sit apart from culture. It is this belief that drives manager's over-reliance on systems on the one hand, and an insufficient understanding of, and emphasis on, workplace culture, on the other. They believe, mistakenly, that compliance with such rules and procedures can be achieved simply by the imposition of systems, while ignoring the crucial cultural dimension. Yet it is the latter that ultimately determines the success or failure of such systems (2000:54)."

To repeat, the cultural perspective does not replace the system perspective, it augments it. No one is saying, "ignore systems, all we need to do is get the culture right"; on the contrary, the right culture is necessary to make safety systems work.

Culture: a characteristic of individuals or groups?

So far, the concepts of culture and safety culture have been left vague. It seems obvious enough that safety culture can be defined, at least in a preliminary way, as "a special case of ... culture, one in which safety has a special place in the concerns of those who work for the organisation" (Hudson, nd:2). But what is culture? If we are to understand the relationship of culture to safety we must explore the meaning of culture in more detail.

Social scientists insist that culture in general, and safety culture in particular, is a characteristic of groups, not of individuals. Organisations may have multiple cultures and cultures may overlap and fragment into subcultures, but always the discussion refers to the characteristics of a group or subgroup, not an individual. Nevertheless there is a tendency in management circles to slip into seeing culture as an individual-level phenomenon.

Consider the following statements made by the safety advisor to one large company, Esso Australia:

"Safety performance has been achieved through an unwavering commitment and dedication from all levels in the organisation to create a safety culture which is genuinely accepted by employees and contractors as one of their *primary core personal values* (quoted in Hopkins, 2000a:74, emphasis added)."

The aim, he said, is to "create a *mindset* that no level of injury (not even first aid) is acceptable" (emphasis added).

Esso draws an interesting implication from this. Since safety is about a mindset, it is something which the individual must cultivate 24 hours a day. It cannot be exclusively about occupational safety but must include safety in the home. Hence Esso's 24-hour safety program. This is how Esso's safety advisor expressed it:

"Real commitment to safety can't be 'turned on' at the entrance gate at the start of the day and left behind at the gate on the way home. Safety and well-being of fellow employees is extended beyond the workplace at Esso. A true commitment to safe behaviour is developed by promoting safety as a full time [ie 24-hour] effort both on and off the job."

What is interesting about this formulation is that it sees a culture as a matter of *individual* attitudes — attitudes which can be cultivated at work, but which in the final analysis are characteristics of individuals, not the organisations to which they belong. As such, the individual can take these attitudes from one context to another, from work to home, for example. This view of culture is widespread in the business world. (For a trenchant critique see Berger, 1999.)

It needs to be pointed out, however, that culture as mindset tends to ignore the latent conditions which underlie every workplace accident, highlighting instead workers' attitudes as the cause of accidents. For example, suppose someone falls down a flight of steps. The idea of culture as mindset leads us to explain the accident in terms of worker carelessness, perhaps the failure to use the hand rail. This ignores the possible contribution of staircase design to the accident. Nevertheless, the approach *is* potentially relevant to minor accidents — slips, trips and falls — which individuals *might* possibly avoid simply by exercising greater care.

However, creating the right mindset among front line workers is not a strategy which can be effective in dealing with hazards about which those workers have no knowledge and which can be identified and controlled only by management, using systematic hazard identification procedures. It is *management* culture rather than the culture of the workforce in general which is most relevant here. If culture is understood as mindset, what is required is a *management* mindset that every significant hazard will be identified and controlled and a *management* commitment to make available whatever resources are necessary to ensure that the workplace is safe.

The content of culture: values or practices?

The Esso statements above make two assumptions about culture. The first, already dealt with, is that culture is essentially an individual-level phenomenon. The second is that culture concerns *attitudes and values*. This second assumption needs critical examination.

Schein (1992:8-9) provides a useful summary of the way the concept of culture has been used by various writers: observed behavioural regularities, group norms, espoused values, formal philosophy, rules of the game, climate, embedded skills, habits of thinking, shared meanings and root metaphors. Some of these usages focus on values, in the way that the Esso statement does, but others stress behaviour as the key element of culture. Of course, behaviour is informed by values, so there is no actual conflict between these usages; it is simply a question of emphasis.

At times Schein himself has emphasised the behavioural element in culture by defining it as "the way we do things around here" (1992:8-9), perhaps the best known of all definitions of culture. This is clearly a definition which highlights *collective practices*. Notice that "the way we do things around here" carries with it the connotation that this is the *right*, or *appropriate* or *accepted* way to do things. These judgments stem necessarily from shared assumptions or values. To reiterate, then, this definition in terms of practices does not deny the importance of values.[1]

Reason adopts this view of culture as collective practices and argues that it is more useful than the idea of culture as values. It is more useful because it provides a practical way to bring about culture change. Practices can be directly affected by management while values cannot. Quoting Hofstede, he writes:

> "Changing collective values of adult people in an intended direction is extremely difficult, if not impossible. Values do change, but not according to someone's master plan. Collective practices, however, depend on organizational characteristics like structures and systems, and can be influenced in more or less predictable ways by changing these (1997:194)."

An example will make the point. Suppose a university is concerned about sexual harassment and wishes to change the culture with respect to such behaviour. It may decide to try to change values directly by putting up posters condemning sexual harassment and urging people to think differently about it. By itself, this is likely to be an ineffective strategy, in part because those whose behaviour is perceived by others as harassing may not themselves perceive it as such. Moreover, if victims of sexual harassment are discouraged from complaining by procedures designed to protect alleged perpetrators from unfair accusations, one can confidently predict that the attempt to change values in this matter will be a failure. If on the other hand the university develops *practices* which support complainants and which

---

1 Schein has more recently modified his formal definition so that it does not include behaviour patterns overtly but refers instead to "shared basic assumptions". The definition is as follows: "The culture of a group can now be defined as a pattern of shared basic assumptions that the group learned as it solved its problems of external adaptation and internal integration, that has worked well enough to be considered valid and, therefore, to be taught to new members as the correct way to perceive, think, and feel in relation to those problems" (p 12). Schein's stated reason for modifying his definition is that not all behavioural regularities are determined by ideas and values; some behaviour may be based on biological reflex reactions, for example. But while not all behaviour patterns are based on shared values, shared values undoubtedly give rise to patterns of behaviour, and it is the job of the cultural analyst to identify the connections between values and behaviour. It is clear, therefore, that Schein is not repudiating his earlier definition of culture in terms of collective practices, merely refining it.

effectively convey to those about whom complaints are made that their behaviour in unacceptable, one can expect successful culture change.

An organisation which focuses its efforts on changing practices is not of course turning its back on value change. Psychology teaches us that human beings feel tension when their behaviour is out of alignment with their values. Such a condition is known as cognitive dissonance (Kahn, 1984:115ff). There is consequently a tendency to bring the two into alignment. If the behaviour is effectively determined by the organisation then the individual's values will shift accordingly. Thus, if an organisation constrains an individual to behave safely, that individual will begin to value safe behaviour more highly. Focusing on practices, therefore, is a not a superficial strategy which leaves the more deep seated aspects of a culture untouched. Changing practices will in the end change values and assumptions as well.

Notice that the idea of culture as collective practices reinforces the idea that culture is specific to a group or organisation, since the practices in one organisation are unlikely to be relevant in their entirety to another. In particular, work practices may be largely inapplicable at home, rendering problematic any idea of 24-hour safety culture.

Culture and leadership

This focus on organisational practices places the responsibility for culture squarely on senior management, for it is the leaders of an organisation who determine how it functions, and it is their decision making which determines, in particular, whether an organisation exhibits the practices which go to make up a culture of safety. Schein puts the point quite strikingly as follows: "Leaders create and change cultures, while managers and administrators live within them" (1992:5). For Schein, the ability to create and change cultures is the defining feature of leaders; it is that which distinguishes them from mere managers. His distinction is exaggerated, but his point is clear enough. If the culture of an organisation is secretive, it is because its leadership has encouraged secretive behaviour; if it is bureaucratic, it is because its leaders have encouraged bureaucratic functioning. There are of course structural limits on the extent to which leaders can change cultures; for example, an army must function hierarchically and it is not within the power of military leaders to democratise military operations. But, within these limits, leaders can define the cultures of their organisations.

How then do leaders create cultures? I turn again to Schein. Leaders create cultures, he says, by "what they systematically pay attention to. This can mean anything from what they notice and comment on to what they measure, control, reward and in others ways systematically deal with" (1992:231). This is such an important statement that it deserves elaboration. Too often, leaders think that they can achieve safe operation by stating publicly that safety comes first and that no job is so important that it cannot be done safely, and then leaving it to others to ensure that the organisation runs safely while they get on with investment, company restructuring and marketing. Some chief executives formalise this systematic lack of attention by stating that it is their job to look outwards, while the job of deputies is to attend to the internal affairs of the organisation. Such leaders express surprise and dismay when they discover, following some major accident, that the organisation for which they are responsible was systematically inattentive to safety, and that the practices of the organisation were geared to maximising production, not safety. According to Schein, however, there is nothing surprising about this; it is a direct outcome of the behaviour modelled by the leadership.

This problem is particularly acute in large multinational companies with diverse portfolios of assets. In these companies the top people are likely to have been appointed for their expertise in financial matters and may know nothing about the technical details of the assets under their control. In these circumstances they may decide to leave safety to others, without realising that in so doing they are inadvertently conveying a message about priorities.

The disaster at the Moura coal mine in central Queensland, which exploded in 1994, killing 11 men, illustrates Schein's point. The inquiry revealed a culture, a set of practices, focused on maximising production and largely oblivious to the potential for explosion. There was one particularly telling example which emerged at the inquiry of the way management attention shaped this culture (Hopkins, 1999:91). Moura was a technically sophisticated mine with a variety of continuous monitoring systems. One of these systems monitored production. Coal was sent to the surface on a conveyer belt and the tonnage coming out of the mine was carefully recorded on a tonnage meter in the manager's office. A second system monitored mine gases and displayed the results on computer screens, enabling observers to monitor changes in mine conditions and determine whether the risk of an explosion was increasing. In short, one system monitored production and the other, safety. On the night of the explosion, the gas monitoring system was indicating a rising potential for explosion, but the manager on duty was not following these trends closely. He *was* monitoring production, however, and noticed from his tonnage meter that production had temporarily ceased. He was on the phone to the miners underground, asking about the hold up, when the explosion occurred. This is perhaps only a vignette, but it is indicative of the systematic attention that was paid to production by managers at Moura and the systematic lack of attention paid to safety. This managerial focus shaped the whole culture of the mine.

This example has an important implication. Organisational cultures may be detrimental to safety, not because leaders have chosen to sacrifice safety for the sake of production, but because they have not focused their attention on safety at all. The converse of this is that if leaders attend to both production and safety, the organisations they lead will exhibit a culture which potentially emphasises both.

Where safety and production *are* in direct conflict, the influence of leadership will again be decisive in setting the priorities. Consider the following case. The manager of a power station which was running at less than full capacity suddenly discovered that the spot price for power had risen sharply. He decided to bring two idle generators on line, without doing the normal checks, in order to take advantage of the high prices on offer. The chief executive of the company which owned the power station happened to be on site that day. When the manager explained to him what he had done, the chief executive thanked the manager for the concern he had shown for the company's interests but instructed him to take the generators back off line, and do the required checks before bringing them into production again. The chief executive knew that this process would take hours and would cost the company hundreds of thousands of dollars in lost revenue, but he also knew that without this intervention he would be conveying a message to the manager that when production requirements conflicted with safety, it was acceptable to take short cuts. His action on this occasion conveyed the priority he wanted given to safety and taught the manager an unforgettable lesson. What he was doing was creating a culture which not only emphasised safety but gave safety priority over production when the two were in conflict.

Leaders who wish to attend systematically to safety, and be seen to be doing so, need to develop some regular safety practices. One critical practice is regular site "walk-arounds" to talk informally with front line staff about safety issues they may be facing. The report on the Ladbroke Grove rail crash in the United Kingdom stressed the importance of this practice:

> "Companies in the rail industry should be expected to demonstrate that they have, and implement, a system to ensure that senior management spend an adequate time devoted to safety issues, with front line workers. ... best practice suggests at least one hour per week should be formally scheduled in the diaries of senior executives for this task. Middle ranking managers should have one hour per day devoted to it, and first line managers should spend at least 30% of their time in the field (Cullen, 2001:64-65)."

There are also further systematic practices senior managers can do on such visits. Here are two suggestions:

1. Familiarise yourself with a safety critical procedure at the site. When you arrive, audit the procedure with scepticism. Imagine ways in which it might be failing and check to see if it is. The famous Piper Alpha disaster in the North Sea in 1988 began with a failure of the permit-to-work system. The system was regularly audited, but never sceptically, and the systematic flaws in the system were never identified. A leader who identifies flaws in a safety critical procedure and instructs that they be corrected will have a powerful effect on the culture at that site. Safety managers can assist their leaders by selecting an appropriate procedure and briefing the leader on its purpose and how it should be working.

2. Familiarise yourself with an accident or near miss, which has occurred at the site and any recommendations which arose from the investigation. When you arrive, speak to the individuals directly concerned, and to all their superiors, up to and including the site manager, about what lessons were learnt and how they have been implemented. If necessary, personally follow up at a later date with the people directly concerned.

The results of a survey in the Australian mining industry in 1999 provide evidence that not enough leaders act in these ways. One survey question was: does management always put safety first? While 84% of senior managers thought they did, only 43% of plant operators agreed. Clearly, lower level employees did not perceive the actions of senior managers as matching their words (Pitzer, 1999:8; see also Shaw and Blewitt, 2000).

Do all organisations have a safety culture?

Having examined the meaning of culture in general, we can now turn to safety culture, in particular. As foreshadowed in the Introduction to this book, a preliminary question to be addressed is whether all organisations can be said to have a safety culture, or only some. Let us consider from this point of view the much quoted definition provided by the International Atomic Energy Agency:

> "[Safety culture is] that assembly of characteristics and attitudes in organisations and individuals which establishes that as an overriding priority, ... safety issues receive the attention warranted by their significance (quoted in Reason, 1997:194)."

It is clear that, according to this definition, by no means all organisations have a safety culture, only those for which safety is an overriding priority. That is certainly Reason's position: "Like a state of grace, a safety culture is something that is striven for but rarely attained" (1997:220). Another prominent writer on this topic, Patrick Hudson, likewise suggests that only after an organisation has passed a certain stage of development in its focus on safety can it be said to have a safety culture (nd:2). Where a safety culture exists in this sense it is appropriate to talk of a culture of safety.

The alternative usage is that all organisations can be said to have a safety culture, which may vary in its effectiveness. On this view, safety cultures which have a strong focus on safety can be distinguished from those with a weaker focus by calling them positive, or full, or true, or strong safety cultures. A great deal of empirical research is premised on this idea that all organisations have a safety culture of sorts, the research objective being to assess, or measure, or investigate the extent which an organisation's safety culture is indeed focused on safety.

Part of the reason for this confusion is to do with language. As Andrew Hale points out (2000:5), safety culture has been treated as largely synonymous with safety climate in the empirical research literature. The two terms have been fighting for supremacy and the trend has been for culture to gain ground at the expense of climate. However, the two have different linguistic consequences. Talk of safety climate and safety climate surveys does not presuppose a climate *favourable* to safety. In contrast, the term safety culture does convey the idea of a culture focused on safety. In short, the English language suggests a distinction between these two terms and to treat them as synonymous creates needless confusion.

Hale's view is that the term safety culture is now so widely used to mean safety climate that there is no alternative but to continue using it in this way and to cope with the confusion. My own inclination is to follow Reason and Hudson and to restrict the term to cultures which indeed emphasise safety. In this book, then, safety culture is treated as a synonym for culture of safety.

The content of a safety culture

If culture in general is to be understood in terms of collective practices, what are the collective practices which make up a safety culture? Reason identifies at least four sets of practices: a reporting culture, a just culture, a learning culture and a flexible culture (1997: Ch 9; see also Hudson, nd).

A reporting culture

Above all else, a safety culture is a reporting culture, in which people are prepared to report errors, near misses, unsafe conditions, inappropriate procedures and any other concerns they may have about safety. The issue is not whether the organisation has a reporting system; it is whether, *as a matter of practice*, such things are reported. This will happen only if people are on the lookout for things which need to be reported and alert to the ways in which things may be going wrong.

A just culture

A reporting culture depends in turn on how the organisation handles blame and punishment. If blame is the routine response to error, then reports will not be forthcoming. If on the other hand blame is reserved for behaviour involving defiance, recklessness or malice, reporting in general will not be discouraged. What is required is not so much a no-blame culture as a just culture.

A learning culture

Reports are effective only if an organisation learns from them. A third feature of a culture of safety, therefore, is that it is a learning culture, one which processes information in a conscientious way and makes changes accordingly.

A flexible culture

Finally, a safety culture is flexible, in the sense that decision-making processes vary, depending on the urgency of the decision and the expertise of the people involved. In short, decisions are made by the people best equipped to make them. This is perhaps not as obvious as the other features discussed above and requires illustration. Decisions about NASA's ill-fated *Colombia* shuttle, and the *Challenger* before it (Vaughan, 1996), were not made by the engineers best equipped to make these decisions, but by senior NASA officials who were protected by NASA's bureaucratic structure from the debates about the wisdom of proposed actions. Had the engineers concerned made these decisions, the disastrous *Challenger* launch would never have occurred and *Columbia's* catastrophic re-entry into the earth's atmosphere would have been handled differently, and probably without loss of life.

This is not the place for an extensive discussion of these four features of a safety culture. Readers interested in further details should consult Reason's book, *Managing the Risks of Organisational Accidents*. My purpose in listing them here is simply to highlight the centrality of collective or organisational practices in Reason's conception of safety culture. This is far cry from the concept of safety as individual "mindset" or "core personal values", discussed earlier.

Collective mindfulness

The second cultural approach to safety comes from research on what are called high reliability organisations (HROs). Organisations such as nuclear power stations and United States aircraft carriers appear to function with remarkable reliability despite the inherent risks, and Karl Weick and his associates argue that what characterises these organisations is their "collective mindfulness" of danger.

Mindfulness is normally thought of as an individual-level phenomenon, so it is important to emphasise that Weick and Sutcliffe see collective mindfulness as a characteristic of organisations. Consider, for instance, the following comment. HROs "organise themselves in such a way that they are better able to notice the unexpected in the making and halt its development" (Weick and Sutcliffe, 2001:3). This is first and foremost a statement about style of organisation, not about the mental state of individuals.

The term collective mindfulness is potentially confusing. It can easily be understood as referring to a group whose members are all individually mindful. In my experience this is what employers assume when they are introduced to the idea, and it is this which sparks their interest. A company whose employees were all individually mindful of risks would be a dream come true for many employers.

Of course, mindful organisations will generate mindful individuals. Furthermore, mindfulness at the individual level is arguably the ultimate goal. Weick and Sutcliffe at times talk about mindful organisations as ones where "people begin to expect mindfulness from one another" (2001:120). But their fundamental point is that individuals will be mindful only if there are processes of mindfulness at the organisational level.

There are clear parallels here with safety culture. The theorists of both safety culture and collective mindfulness insist that these are group-level phenomena. On the other hand, employers tend to focus at the level of the individual and would love to be able to inculcate safety awareness or mindfulness directly into the consciousness of their workforces.

The processes of mindful organising

The truly organisational nature of collective mindfulness becomes apparent when we examine some of what Weick and Sutcliffe describe as the processes of mindful organising, given below.

1. Preoccupation with failure

Mindful organisations understand that long periods of success breed complacency and they are therefore wary of success. They are preoccupied with the possibility of failure. They hunt for lapses, errors and incongruencies, recognising that these may be the precursors to larger failures. They therefore have well-developed systems for reporting near misses, process upsets and small and localised failures of all sorts. In Reason's terms they have well-developed reporting cultures.

2. Reluctance to simplify

All organisations must simplify the data which confront them in order to make decisions and move forward. Simplification means discarding some information as unimportant or irrelevant. But this is inherently dangerous, for the discarded information may be the very information necessary to avert disaster. "Simplifications increase the likelihood of eventual surprise" (Weick and Sutcliffe, 2001:94). Mindful organisations are therefore reluctant to discard information. "They position themselves to see as much as possible" (Weick and Sutcliffe, 2001:11). They socialise their workforces to notice more and they employ more people whose job it is to explore complexity and to double check on claims of competency and of success. Cost-cutting organisations regard such people as redundant and work on the assumption that redundancy is the enemy of efficiency. Mindful organisations treat redundancy as vital for the collection and interpretation of information which is necessary to avert disaster.

3. Sensitivity to operations

A crucial feature of mindful organisations is that their front line operators strive to maintain situational awareness, or sensitivity to operations; that is, they strive to remain as aware as possible of the current state of operations. Moreover, they strive to understand the implications of the present situation for future functioning. All this presupposes front line operators who are highly informed about operations as a whole, about how operations can fail and about strategies for recovery.

It is not only front line operators who must be sensitive to operations. Managers must be sensitive to the experience of their front line operators, in particular by encouraging them to report on their experiences. Weick and Sutcliffe note that "people who refuse to speak up out of fear enact a system that knows less than it needs to know to remain effective" (2001:13). This is precisely the point which Reason makes in talking about the importance of a no-blame culture, or more accurately, a just culture.

4. Commitment to resilience and deference to expertise

According to Weick, Sutcliffe and Obstfeld, mindful organisations show a commitment to resilience, by which they mean that they are not disabled by errors or crises but mobilise themselves in special ways when these events occur so as to be able to deal with them. For example, "knowledgeable people self-organise into ad hoc networks to provide expert problem solving. These networks, which have no formal status, dissolve as soon as normalcy returns" (1999:100). Thus, air traffic controllers, at times of peak activity, may group themselves around a single screen to give advice and backup to the controller in the hot seat.

Related to this is the deference to expertise. When operations are being carried out at very high tempo, the locus of decision-making "migrates" to the people with the greatest expertise or knowledge about the events in question. These people may be relatively low in the hierarchy, but at such times, more senior managers will defer to their expertise. Researchers have identified this as a consistent pattern in flight operations on aircraft carriers, for example. When the tempo returns to normal, authority moves back up the hierarchy. Reason refers to this as a flexible culture.

The relationship between safety culture and organisational mindfulness

It is clear from this account of the processes of mindful organising that safety culture and organisational mindfulness are closely related ideas. Both concepts refer in the first instance to organisational — not individual — level characteristics. Moreover, both are avowedly cultural concepts. Weick and Sutcliffe themselves speak of a "culture of mindfulness" and its relationship to safety culture in the following passage:

> "... the concept of safety culture illuminates what it means to create a culture of mindfulness ... Our interest in safety cultures stems (in part) ... from their concern with mindfulness (2001:127)."

Even at the level of detail, there is a surprising agreement between the practices which go to make up a safety culture and the list of practices which Weick and Sutcliffe see as characterising mindful organisations. It should be noted, finally, that writers in both traditions recognise that the state they advocate is rare, and it is probably fair to say that both concepts are ideals against which real organisations can be measured, rather than descriptions which apply in their entirety to any organisation.

The need for risk-awareness

The third approach to culture and safety uses risk-awareness as its conceptual lynch pin. As we shall see, risk-awareness is synonymous with mindfulness, so this is simply an alternative way of approaching the same set of ideas.

The rationale for encouraging risk-awareness among employees stems in part from the impossibility of devising a set of safety rules which adequately covers every situation. A striking example of this problem came to light a few years ago in the New South Wales underground coal mine industry. Mining is carried out in many mines by large mining machines, called continuous miners, which are controlled by mine workers standing a few feet away, using a hand held "remote". The machines have devices which reinforce the roof as they progress, but there will always be potentially dangerous areas of unsupported roof in the vicinity. The government inspectorate had therefore promulgated rules prohibiting workers from standing under unsupported roof. Studies revealed that these requirements were being routinely violated and the explanation was that the miner drivers faced many risks not envisaged in the rules, and that balancing these risks required them on occasions to stand under unsupported roof. Among these additional risks were: falls of coal from the side walls, being pinched between the mining machine and the wall as the machine swivelled, being hit by the trailing power cable, and being hit from behind by an approaching shuttle car. The rules failed to take account of all the hazards in the environment and were therefore inappropriate.

It is tempting to think that the problem might be overcome by a more detailed set of rules which dealt with all the risks involved. But it seems likely that the mining situation described above is so complex that no rules will be adequate. Clearly, the work process in which these drivers are involved needs to be redesigned, to eliminate some of the risks. But what this example suggests is that workers will inevitably find themselves confronted at times with situations in which the rules are inadequate, or inapplicable, and discretion must be exercised. In these situations they need to act with a heightened awareness of the risks involved.

There is no implication here, however, that safety can be achieved by abandoning rules in favour of a strategy of risk-awareness. Rules provide certainty about what must be done in particular situations, and they are an important resource in the struggle against all-pervasive commercial pressures to take risks (Berger, 1999).

The fact that rules are essential but can never be complete brings us to something of an impasse. One way to move beyond this impasse is to abandon the idea that a set of rules can ever be determined once and for all, and to recognise that a regime of rules is necessarily a dynamic one, which needs to be *managed*. This idea has been extensively developed by Hale and his colleagues (2003). They propose that the management of safety rules includes the following steps:

1. Rules must be initially developed with the input of end users as well as other experts. End users are expert in the daily situations which confront them, but the expertise of others is necessary to take account of possibilities of which end users may not be aware. Decisions about how rules are to be enforced must also be determined at this stage.

2. Rules must be trialled to ensure their practicability and intelligibility, and they must be approved by relevant parties at various levels before being promulgated.

3. Rules must then be effectively communicated and people must be trained.

4. Once introduced, rules must be monitored, deviations responded to, and decisions made about whether rules need to be modified.

5. Finally, there must be a rule modification process which cycles through these steps again.

Steps 4 and 5 ensure that the rule regime is never fixed but is able to evolve as circumstances dictate. Hale and his colleagues note that very few organisations give any emphasis to steps 4 and 5 and the result is that their rule regimes lack a self-corrective mechanism and may become obsolete or ineffective as situations change. (See also Lawton, 1998; Leplat, 1998; and Simard and Marchand, 1997.)

The idea that rules must be managed acknowledges implicitly that rules may be imperfect and that complying with an existing rule may not always provide the best guarantee of safety. It invites end users to be alert to the need for rule changes. It invites them, in other words, to attend to the risks they face and not simply to comply with rules in a mindless fashion. In this way, the idea that safety rules must be managed incorporates the need for risk-awareness, rather than replacing it.

Promoting risk-awareness

To be effective, risk-awareness must operate at both the organisational and individual level. But just as safety culture and mindfulness are often seen as characteristics of individuals, so too is risk-awareness sometimes reduced to the mindset of individuals. The Minerals Council of Australia, for example, defines awareness as "the state of mind where we are constantly aware of the possibility of injury and act accordingly at all times". The point is, however, that risk-awareness among individuals is crucially dependent on the organisational context. As employees become more risk-aware they are more likely to report matters of concern and more likely to make suggestions for safety improvements. If the organisation is one which discourages reporting and fails to act on information and suggestions coming from its workforce, employees will quickly become disillusioned. The risk-awareness strategy will then be viewed as an attempt to transfer responsibility for safety from the employer to the employee and to blame workers for being insufficiently risk-aware when things go wrong. If, on the other hand, the promotion of risk-awareness among employees goes hand in hand with a commitment to risk-awareness at the organisational level, reliable and safe functioning becomes a real possibility.

How, then, can individual risk-awareness be developed? Esso is one company which has embraced the goal of risk-awareness, with its "step back five by five" program. The idea is that before starting a new job, the employee should take five steps back, metaphorically, and take five minutes to think about what might go wrong and how this might be avoided.[2] Esso Norway uses an interesting variant of this idea in its offshore drilling operations. Prior to any job, such as a crane lifting operation, workers may be asked to name two specific barriers or risk control measures which will be used in the operation. The answer might be that radio communication is confirmed and proper hand signals are used in a direct line of sight with the crane operator (Esso Norway team, 2004:3). A further variant is to ask employees to identify three ways in

---

2   The Western Australian Government ran a similar program called "Thinksafe SAM". SAM is
      short for: Spot the hazard, Assess the risk, Make the change.

which things might go wrong and the steps which will be taken to ensure that these unwanted outcomes do not occur. This practice has been recommended to Air Force pilots doing risk-assessments prior to sorties.[3]

Defensive driver training is another interesting example of an attempt to make people more risk-aware. Defensive driving is about anticipating what might go wrong, and taking preventive action before it does. For example, when driving in long queues of cars, watching the brake lights of cars two or more ahead can help prevent highway pileups. Defensive drivers are trained to anticipate mistakes or erratic behaviour by other drivers and to drive accordingly.

But, as has already been made clear, urging employees to comply with such requirements is not enough; organisational practices must encourage the required mental approach. One company that has taken the extra step is Western Mining Corporation (WMC). It has a strategy similar to Esso's called "take time, take charge", which aims to get people to stop, think and then take some appropriate action. What makes this happen is that supervisors are required to ask workers each day to tell them of instances where they have taken time and taken charge. What makes *this* happen is that, at weekly meetings with managers, supervisors are asked to provide examples of take time, take charge that have been reported to them. There is also feedback to original reporters in cases which are judged to be of significance. WMC has an employee at the corporate level whose full-time job is to supervise the whole process (WMC has about 4000 employees), a clear indication of the company's commitment to make this set of practices work. Notice that risk-awareness among front line employees is the aim, but the focus of the program is on the behaviour of managers and supervisors. It is the practices at this level which determine the success or otherwise of the strategy. A culture of risk-awareness will not be brought about simply by preaching its virtues; practices which encourage it must be embedded within the organisation.

Cultures of risk-denial

In many circumstances organisations and individuals are not simply unaware of risks; there are mechanisms that deny the existence of risk. Sometimes these are so well developed that they can be described as cultures of risk-denial. It will be convenient here to describe the culture of denial as a set of beliefs, but of course, as discussed earlier, there will necessarily be practices which go with each of these beliefs and give expression to them.

Research into major accidents reveals that there were always warning signs, prior to the occurrence, whose significance was missed or dismissed. A culture of risk-denial is often the culprit. The elements of such cultures are remarkably

---

3   Consultancy work by the author.

similar from one accident to another and I shall illustrate the idea by reference to the Gretley coal mine disaster in New South Wales in 1996 in which four men died (Hopkins, 2000b). Mining was taking place at Gretley in the vicinity of old, abandoned, flooded workings. Miners were getting closer to the old workings and water was seeping out of the mine face as they worked. This was a warning that they might be dangerously close. The warnings were ignored and miners eventually broke through into the old workings, water rushed in and four men were drowned. The specific beliefs which facilitated risk-denial in this case were as follows.

The belief that it can't happen here

Management at Gretley had obtained plans of the location of the old workings and intended to work at a safe distance. The plans were in error and the workings were 100 metres closer than the plans indicated. Because management was relying on the accuracy of the old plans, it felt entitled to dismiss the warning signs. Management's view was: "We know about the hazard in question, but we have it under control so the warnings we are getting can be ignored." This is a common belief in cultures of risk-denial, lulling all concerned into a false sense of security.

Normalising the evidence

On various occasions mine safety officers reported the water leaking out of the mine face in their end of shift reports. One of these reports, for example, stated: "coal seam giving out a considerable amount of water seepage". Mine managers read these reports but dismissed their significance on the grounds that this was a wet mine, which it was, and that water seepage was therefore to be expected. In this way, events which might have been interpreted as warnings of danger were normalised, allowing them to be ignored.

This process by which adverse events are normalised has been noted before as an important precursor to disaster. Vaughan (1996) describes it in her discussion of the space shuttle, *Challenger*, which caught fire and plunged to earth in 1986, killing the seven astronauts on board. The integrity of the rockets depended on certain rubber seals, known as O-rings. It had been discovered on several previous launches that they did not perform as required at low temperatures. In fact, they malfunctioned. Nevertheless, they had not failed totally. Over time the malfunctioning was reconceptualised as normal and the risk of total failure came to be judged acceptably low. (Vaughan describes this as the "normalisation of deviance".) The temperature on launch day was colder than at previous launches. But the technical malfunction had been normalised. The launch was thus given the go-ahead. This time the seals failed totally, with catastrophic results.

Ad hoc criteria

In rejecting the significance of the trickle of water coming from the face at Gretley, the mine manager noted that water was merely "seeping out", "not squirting out of the face like water pistols". In so doing he had implicitly defined a new test for danger: water squirting out of the face under high pressure is an indication of danger; a trickle is not. No justification was provided for this new test. The structure of this argument is, first, to define a higher threshold criterion for what constitutes danger. Then, since the higher threshold has not been crossed, the warning signs can be dismissed.

The downgrading of intermittent warnings

Many warning signs are intermittent in nature, which can lead observers to downgrade their significance. The trickle of water from the face in the days prior to the inrush was observable only when the area was undisturbed; when coal was being cut and loaded, no water could be seen. This appeared to alleviate whatever concerns there might have been in the minds of miners themselves. There was nothing rational about this; it was very much a case of out of sight, out of mind.

The onus of proof

At Gretley, it was possible to interpret the water seepage either as something to be expected in a naturally wet mine, or as an indicator that mining was dangerously close to the old workings. Management chose the former interpretation. The view appeared to be that unless the signs conclusively established danger, the mine could be presumed safe.

A very similar mindset prevailed at the time of the *Challenger* launch. Management had discussed the O-ring issue and asked for conclusive evidence that the O-rings would not work. The engineers could not provide this evidence. It was therefore presumed that the O-rings would work. In this way the doubt was resolved in favour of a decision to launch.

When a doubt is raised about the safety of an operation, is it up to those who raise the doubt to establish that a danger exists, or is it up to those conducting the operation to prove that it is safe? Where does the onus of proof lie? In risk-denying cultures, safety is assumed until danger is proved.

Groupthink

Where warning signs are detected, a small group will sometimes be assembled to evaluate their significance. There is an unspoken presumption that decision making in small groups will be consensual, indeed unanimous. The result is that doubters often feel constrained to concur with the dominant risk-denying view. Moreover, because the process is one of collective decision making, those advocating the risk-denying position can do so knowing that they will not be held personally responsible should the decision turn out to be wrong.

The phenomenon has been described as groupthink (Janis, 1972) and it has played a role in many disastrous decisions, including the *Challenger* launch decision. There are practices which can be employed to counter the influence of groupthink (Stephan, 2001); for example, the designation of one person in the group as the devil's advocate, with the job of opposing the group consensus, but risk-denying cultures make no use of such precautionary practices.

These are some of the features of organisational cultures which deny risk. They are not all present in every risk-denying culture, and there are no doubt other beliefs not mentioned here which can be identified in some such cultures. But wherever we encounter an extensive set of beliefs which serve to undermine the significance of warning signs, it is appropriate to speak of a culture of risk-denial.

Organisations which strive for risk-awareness must overcome these beliefs. They must take warnings seriously no matter how tenuous, intermittent or ambiguous. They must avoid dismissing them as normal and to be expected, and when faced with uncertain information, they should default to a presumption of danger rather than a presumption of safety. If they succeed in this respect they will be truly risk-aware organisations.

Conclusion

It is obvious now that the concepts of safety culture, mindfulness and risk-awareness are largely interchangeable. The choice of one or other of these concepts is therefore largely a matter of linguistic style. All refer to the aspects of organisational culture which are conducive to safety. The important point which has been made is that all operate at both the individual and the organisational level and any attempt by managers or policy makers to stress the individual aspect at the expense of the organisational will be self-defeating.

This chapter has also paid close attention to the meaning of culture in an organisational context. This enables us to go beyond the issue of safety culture and to consider a broader question: how does a particular organisational culture, a particular way of doing things, influence safety? The studies in Parts B and C of this book take up this question in particular organisational settings.

part B

Railway Culture and Safety:
The Glenbrook Train Crash

Chapter 2
Introduction to the Glenbrook case study

In December 1999, a busy commuter train bringing people from the Blue Mountains to work in Sydney arrived at a red light at Glenbrook station, and stopped. The driver had already been told that the light was probably defective and that it had gone to red as a fail safe mechanism, so he radioed the signaller and asked:

"I'm right to go past it, am I, mate?"

Minutes earlier, the *Indian Pacific*, on the last leg of its journey from Perth to Sydney, had been authorised to pass this same signal. However, it had stopped just over a kilometre ahead at a second red light. The signaller did not know that the *Indian Pacific* had stopped, and he replied to the driver of the commuter train:

"Yeah, mate, you certainly are."

The commuter train accelerated away, but upon rounding a bend the driver was aghast to see the interstate train in his way. He applied the emergency breaks and ran back through the carriage warning people of the impending crash. He survived, but seven of his passengers did not.

The conversation reported above had been routinely recorded, and all those who subsequently listened to the recording were shocked by the casual language and careless tone of the interchange.[1] Such a conversation would be unheard of in air traffic control, for example, and expert commentators said they had never heard such ill-disciplined safety-critical communication (McInerney, 2001:82). Communication theorists naturally focused on this as the cause of the accident and suggested that the style of communication may have contributed to a misunderstanding between the driver and signaller. According to one, terms like "buddy" and "mate" lead to "a sort of coded understanding" between those using them. "It's a code for saying, we know that sometimes this doesn't mean what it says ... that we are sharing the same sort of understanding about the ambiguity of the sign" (Thomas, 2000).

But there was no misunderstanding, no ambiguity and certainly no element of collusion here. The driver requested authorisation to proceed and the signaller provided it. Both parties were clear that this is what had happened and

---

1   The complete conversation is reproduced in Chapter 4.

formalising the interchange above would not have made any difference. Had the signaller provided the driver with additional information about the whereabouts of the *Indian Pacific*, the outcome would have been different, but that is not a matter to do with the style of communication, but rather the content. The failure to provide this additional content will be examined later.

The whole purpose of the signalling system is to keep trains apart. How could it fail so catastrophically on this occasion? The public clamoured for answers. Shortly before this accident the New South Wales Government had broken up a unified rail system, run by the State Rail Authority, into a number of government-owned entities which were supposed to run on commercial lines, and there was some suspicion that this fragmentation and commercialisation of the rail system was the fundamental cause of this accident.

In response to the public concern, the Government set up an inquiry under the direction of retired judge Peter McInerney.[2] The inquiry provides an ideal opportunity to explore the themes of this book. The concept of culture was pivotal in the inquiry, both during the hearings and in the final report. The report's central conclusion was that disaggregation of the rail system had destroyed an existing safety culture and the re-creation of a safety culture was "fundamental to achieving an optimum level of safety" (McInerney, 2001:35-36). The hearings themselves were full of references to culture, not all of them helpful. At one point, for example, counsel suggested that the reason train drivers go through red lights is cultural:

> "Commissioner: When one drives a motor car, one doesn't drive through a red light but yet for some reason or other, we have this problem of train drivers going through red lights. To me I find that very difficult to understand ...
>
> Counsel: That has to be cultural behaviour.
>
> Commissioner: I can't understand why it would be cultural behaviour. That is what I am trying to grasp.
>
> Counsel: If you drive in Italy, not that I have done that, it is a bit like the railways; you stop at the light, if you stop at all. And you just keep going through it. It's just a slight hick-up in some of these countries, in the culture and behaviour.
>
> Commissioner: In Italy?
>
> Counsel: They don't stop at red lights.[3]"

---

2   *Special Commission of Inquiry into the Glenbrook Rail Accident.*

3   References to the transcript will not be provided here. Details will be provided on request.

Counsel was very wide of the mark with this analogy. It may or may not be true that Italian car drivers have a culture of ignoring red lights, but train drivers in New South Wales certainly do not. The commuter train driver stopped at the light and proceeded only when he was authorised to do so. Counsel's analysis is facile in the extreme and it is easy to see how arguments of this sort can give cultural analysis a bad name. Fortunately the Commissioner did not accept this analysis.

It is not simply the fact that the word "culture" figures prominently in the inquiry that makes the case so interesting. It is that the inquiry gives us a detailed picture of an organisational culture and the practices that made up that culture. It was a culture which focused primarily on getting passengers to their destinations on time — on time running — and it did this very successfully. But it was also a culture insensitive to risk — indeed, given to the denial of risk — with the result that employees lacked any awareness or knowledge of risk.

The inappropriateness of blame

Judicial inquiries into major accidents are often seen by the parties concerned as an exercise is allocating or, alternatively, ducking blame. The rail track owner, an organisation which, as we shall see later, bore some responsibility for the accident, argued that the driver of the commuter train was solely to blame, because he was driving too fast. According to counsel for the track owner, his speed, in the circumstances, was "quite extraordinary". On the other hand, counsel for the deceased passengers argued that the signaller and a train controller had shown "reckless indifference" to their jobs. This is strong language in a legal context for it is tantamount to saying that they should be charged with murder.

Errors by front line personnel are hardly an adequate explanation for why something went wrong. There is no doubt that the signaller made a monumental error in authorising the driver to pass the first signal. We need to ask, *why* did this error occur? How could he be so oblivious to the whereabouts of the interstate train and so unaware of the possibility of collision? Moreover, the train driver, once authorised to pass the red signal, was supposed to observe certain speed restrictions. He failed to do so. This was not just an error, it was a violation. Again, we need to ask, *why* did he violate the rule as flagrantly as he did?

Asking *why* errors were made is far more useful than asking *who* is to blame. Asking *why* leads invariably to more fundamental cultural and organisational causes. Inquiries must get to this level if they are to be of any value in preventing recurrences. Moreover, once it is understood that there are reasons why people behave as they do, blame becomes far less appropriate. Pursuing these reasons here will enable us to build up a picture of the culture of the railways and how it contributed to the accident.

The Commissioner, himself, was not concerned with allocating blame and saw his function as identifying causes so as to be able to make appropriate recommendations for the prevention of future accidents. He became very frustrated with the single-minded focus of the rail organisations in pointing the finger of blame at others, and he commented scathingly on their lack of helpfulness when it came to making recommendations for the future.

The organisation of Part B

Part B of this book, then, is an inquiry into the culture of the New South Wales railways and how this organisational culture undermined safety and contributed to the Glenbrook crash. I take seriously the idea that culture is a set of practices and so we shall be examining the practices which go to make up the railway culture, not simply the ideas in people's minds, as discussions of culture so often do.[4] Four main constellations of practices and hence four cultural themes were revealed in the inquiry. The chapters which follow are organised around these themes.

First, this was very much a rule-focused culture. A great deal of effort went into rule making, with the result that employees were overwhelmed with safety rules — eight volumes of them. This focus on rules tended to deaden awareness of risks. Moreover, when accidents occurred, the aim of accident investigations appeared to be to identify which rules had been violated and by whom. The obsession with rules led, therefore, to a pronounced tendency to blame.

Second, the railway system was organisationally and occupationally fragmented. The organisational fragmentation was a result of the commercialisation of the system in 1996, but the occupational gulf that existed between signallers, drivers and rail workers predated this change. I have called this aspect of the way things were done, a culture of "silos". The result was a failure of people to recognise that their actions or inactions might have implications for the safety of people in other parts of the system.

Third, there was a powerful culture of punctuality — of on time running. This was maintained with a host of practices, and studying just how the railways went about achieving on time running provides a key to how organisations might go about achieving an equivalently powerful culture of safety. The culture of on time running was in many respects an admirable aspect of railway culture, but its side effect was to undermine safety.

---

4   See the discussion in Part A.

Fourth, the railway culture was profoundly risk-blind, even risk-denying. In a host of ways it turned its back on safety and gave priority to other goals; in particular, on time running. The inquiry generated a great deal of debate about how railways in particular and organisations in general can create cultures of risk-awareness. Some important ideas emerged and will be examined here.

Finally, I argue that the rail culture disempowered its employees and that a culture of empowerment is a precondition for risk-awareness at both the organisational and individual levels.

The cultural themes discussed here are those which emerged during the inquiry into the Glenbrook rail crash. The study of organisational cultures in other contexts would no doubt yield different constellations of practices, and no doubt, too, readers familiar with other organisations will note certain similarities. Recent inquiries into rail crashes in the United Kingdom reveal remarkable similarities between the cultural themes in that context and those identified here. These will be alluded to at some points in the following chapters.

One of the major challenges facing authors is how to organise the material to be presented. I have organised it here around cultural themes. But this is not the only way the material might have been assembled. Had the purpose been simply to tell the story of the Glenbrook train crash, or to evaluate the impact of disaggregation, a different principle of organisation would have been adopted. One consequence of the way I have chosen to organise the material here is that the reader is not provided with a systematic account of the accident in the way that was done in my earlier publication, *Lessons from Longford*, for example. Readers interested in such an account should consult the official Glenbrook report, which is very easy to read. Alternatively, an overview of the causal factors discussed here is presented in a diagram in Chapter 7.

This analysis of the Glenbrook rail crash draws largely on the three-volume report of the official inquiry and the 5000 pages of transcript. The inquiry and the report provide a remarkable insight into the thinking of people in organisations which lack an awareness of risk. It is a case study which enriches our understanding of how organisational cultures affect safety.

Chapter 3
A culture of rules

Once authorised to pass the red light, the commuter train driver set off at a cracking pace. According to safety rule 245, which governed the authorised passing of red signals, he was supposed to proceed with extreme caution, and in such a way that he could stop short of any obstruction on the track. The driver did not comply with this requirement. He accelerated to about 50 kilometres per hour. The normal maximum speed for this rather curved section of the track was 60 kilometres per hour, so the driver had clearly reduced his speed somewhat in light of the circumstances. In fact, he was driving in such a way that he could stop at the next signal, should it be red. Unfortunately, however, he was driving much too fast to be able to stop short of any obstruction on the track and hence was unable to stop in time when he saw the back end of the *Indian Pacific* ahead. Had he been complying strictly with the rule, the accident would not have occurred, and this was the basis on which various parties at the inquiry sought to hold him responsible.

This brief description highlights the railways' reliance on rules as a means of averting accidents. The belief was that it was possible to create a set of rules which covered every risky situation employees might encounter. Safety would then be assured, provided people followed the rules. The failure of signals for technical reasons was one such situation which had been foreseen. Lights were designed to go to red in the event of a failure, but it would clearly be sensible to allow trains to proceed past failed lights, and rule 245 was aimed at allowing this to occur, safely.

This chapter will explore the heavy emphasis which the railways placed on rules as a means of managing risk. It will highlight, in particular, the inability of this culture to instil an awareness of risks in railway employees.

To identify a set of rules which covered every situation was of course an illusory goal, as the railways' own experience demonstrated. In railways in Australia and overseas, accidents historically have been attributed to one of two causes: either the driver or some other employee has failed to observe the rules, in which case some form of discipline might be appropriate, or the rules themselves have proved inadequate. In the latter case, a rule is amended or a new rule developed to fill the hole which has been revealed in the tapestry of rules. The result is that over the years the set of rules becomes more and more bulky and, by the time of the Glenbrook accident, the rule book in New South Wales ran to eight volumes. Amendments were circulated on a weekly basis in cellophane covers and recipients were expected to update their manuals.

They often did not do so and one driver spoke at the inquiry of returning seven years' worth of unopened amendments to his employer at the time of retirement (McInerney, 2001:127). The rate at which rule changes were promulgated was extraordinary. One witness accumulated a pile of unopened amendments two-feet thick in the course of one year. The sheer volume of rules, then, made them virtually unknowable, undermining any value they may have had as a guide to action on a daily basis. The irony was that only the people whose job it was to develop and amend rules had any chance of keeping abreast of them. A more Kafkaesque situation is hard to imagine.

In any case, the rules were not in a user-friendly form. They were written in complex and convoluted ways designed to cover all the possibilities which occurred to the rule writer. This meant that people seeking guidance from the rule would need to sift through all the possibilities listed to see if the situation which confronted them was included. Each rule might be several pages long and read much like a piece of legislation, the meaning of which could be discerned only by careful study, cross-referencing one part of the rule with another, and even cross-referencing one rule with another, to determine just what was the appropriate course of action in the circumstances. Given that many rail workers have limited literacy, these rules might as well have been in a foreign language.

Even for people who applied their minds diligently to interpreting the rules, they could remain quite ambiguous. Workers were given training in the rules, but sometimes even the trainers did not know what the rules meant. Debates in the training room would ensue and the trainer would finally leave the room, ring the people responsible for writing the rule and return to the class room to deliver judgement on the intended meaning of the rule. Further ambiguities arose when there was more than one rule which appeared to apply. In one situation, no fewer than 84 rules were relevant and employees needed to know them all in order to select the correct course of action (McInerney, 2001:72,131).

Finally, because the rules were written by people who had no direct experience of the circumstances to which they applied, they were sometimes wildly impracticable. As the report noted, in some cases the rules were "so restrictive that they were incapable of being applied in operational situations and operational staff had no alternative but to violate the rules to get the job done" (McInerney, 2001:20).

These points were conceded at the inquiry by a former chief executive of the State Rail Authority, who recommended that future rules should be developed in consultation with those who would have to apply them to ensure that they were both understandable and capable of being applied.

The fact that the rules were so often ambiguous and difficult to interpret invites attention to the rule-making process itself. Rule making in some contexts is essentially a political process, the resultant rule being designed to achieve agreement among interested parties. At universities, for example, rules have emerged which require staff to consult students about assessment procedures. Such requirements are totally impractical for large classes, but, in the staff/student committees which formulate these rules, such issues must be glossed over if consensus is to be achieved.

Very little evidence about rule making in the New South Wales railways was given at the inquiry, but it seems quite likely that some such process was at work. It was submitted at one point that the railway safety rules were similar to industrial awards, which are essentially based on bargains struck between the parties. Ambiguity in these circumstances is almost inevitable and may indeed be the price of agreement. The report on the Southall rail crash in the United Kingdom raised this possibility quite explicitly as an explanation for similar problems with rules in the United Kingdom rail system:

> "A possible explanation for rules having been allowed to remain in a state of patent and known ambiguity for so long is that they were thought to reflect a range of different views, in the same way that a political document might be allowed to mean different things in different circumstances (Uff, 2000:201)."

It is not surprising then that workers had little use for these rules (McInerney, 2001:115,116,130,132). They regarded training sessions as all "chalk and talk" and they often went away from training sessions feeling they had no idea of the purpose behind the rules. According to one witness, it was like learning a poem by heart, without understanding its meaning. The rules themselves were seen as "incredible waffle". The result was that workers developed their own rules on the job. One driver was asked at the inquiry if the formal rules were of any assistance in driving trains. His answer: "Not really. Most drivers rely on a hard core of knowledge and years of experience." Another driver told the inquiry he could see no relationship between the content of his training and what he was actually doing on the job. Moreover, the experience-based rules that drivers in fact relied upon seemed, on the whole, to work, and one witness argued that accidents occurred when new drivers, who hadn't had sufficient experience to draw on, tried to rely on formal rules which they did not understand. The Commissioner endorsed this view:

> "The reason for the relative safety of the New South Wales rail industry until recent years has not been due to the success of the rule based approach to rail safety, but more to the fact that employees acquired their knowledge of safe working from experienced employees in the course of serving long periods of formal and informal on the job training (McInerney, 2001:22)."

Not only were the formal rules difficult to apply, but there seemed to be little will to enforce some of them in the normal course of events. An inspector suggested to the inquiry that the speed limit implied in rule 245 was regularly violated because it was inappropriate. He himself recognised it to be inappropriate. He acknowledged, however, that if it were formally bought to his attention that a driver was exceeding the limit he would have no alternative but to advise the driver formally to comply with the rule. The Commissioner thereupon commented as follows: "I think I am getting the message that what the rule says doesn't matter much ... It is coming out loud and clear I think."[1] It would seem that rail inspectors were turning a blind eye to rule violations they knew to be occurring because of the impracticality of the rules.

Rule 245: passing an automatic signal at stop

Rule 245 exemplified all the problems discussed above. It was four pages long and it was addressed to three categories of people: signallers, hand signallers and drivers. Here is the first complexity: these people must sift through the rule to work out which parts applied specifically to them. The rule involved a complex decision tree for drivers: is the signal fitted with a train stop?;[2] is the train fitted with a trip valve?;[3] can the driver see that the line ahead is unoccupied?; is there a hand signaller on site?; can the driver contact the signaller at the control centre?; and is there a disabled train ahead which is in need of assistance? A diagrammatic representation of this decision tree might have helped drivers work through these issues, but no such tree was provided. Instead, the rule was phrased as a confusing set of "either"s, "or"s and "and"s, which made it difficult to interpret even after close study.[4] Theoretically, drivers needed to work through these questions because the correct course of action depended on just which set of circumstances applied: one possibility after stopping was to set off again immediately, a second was to wait a minute and then proceed, while a third was to contact the signaller and proceed according to instructions.

Rule 245 noted that the failure of the signal was not the only reason why it might be at red. It could be that there was a train stopped on the line ahead, or that there was a broken rail in the next section of track. For this reason, trains which passed signals at red were required to proceed at reduced speed. The

---

1 Quotations drawn from the transcript, as this one is, will not be referenced.

2 A train stop is a device on the track, a little distance before a signal, which can automatically apply the train's brakes if the train has not slowed sufficiently to be able to stop at a red signal.

3 A trip valve is a device on a train which enables a train stop to operate the train's brakes.

4 Rule 245 is included in the Appendix. The interested reader is invited to try to work out the meaning of the first page of the rule.

rule required drivers to "proceed with *extreme caution* to the first signal ahead of the signal at stop, [be] *prepared to stop short of any obstruction*, and obey the indication of that signal". Even if that signal was green, the driver was expected to "proceed with extreme caution to the *second* signal ahead of the signal at stop" (emphasis added).

What, then, was the appropriate speed? Some obstructions, such as a broken rail, might be so small that anything faster than walking pace would be too fast to enable a train to be stopped short of the obstruction. Was walking pace the appropriate speed? And what did "extreme caution" mean? This phrase was not defined in the rule and witnesses at the inquiry offered contrasting interpretations. One rail manager stated that indeed it meant walking speed; that is, between three and five kilometres per hour. One of the rail trainers told the inquiry his advice to trainees was that it meant ten kilometres an hour. The driver of the *Indian Pacific*, who had been authorised to pass the defective signal a few minutes before the commuter train, believed that 18 kilometres per hour was consistent with extreme caution. In short, there was a great deal of uncertainty about the speed limit implied in the rule.

Moreover, if the rule makers had intended trains to travel at walking speed every time they encountered a failed signal, they were clearly ignorant of the circumstances confronting drivers. In the metropolitan area where signals are close together, travelling between a pair of signals at walking speed might not constitute a significant delay. But in country areas where signals were further apart, the delays might be intolerable. The distance from the failed Glenbrook signal and the next signal up the line was over a kilometre and it would have taken nearly 20 minutes for a train travelling at walking speed to cover the distance (McInerney, 2000a:20,27-28). The second signal ahead was a further two kilometres up the track and to proceed at walking speed over this second section of track would have taken perhaps another half an hour. For a peak hour commuter train, such a delay would be a major disruption to the schedule, affecting all following trains and potentially inconveniencing thousands of passengers. The rule was quite insensitive to this situation, reflecting the fact that it had been drafted by people remote from the operational realities.

There was a further significant problem with the rule. If another train has passed over the track since a signal has gone to red, and has done so without problem, it can be assumed that there is nothing wrong with the track. Limiting trains to walking speed in these circumstances is quite unnecessary. The Commissioner found that rule 245 was "not appropriate to the circumstances of consecutive trains passing an automatic signal at stop". He went further to say that the driver found himself in a situation in which there was "no applicable" rule (McInerney, 2000a:74). This was not strictly speaking true, but the statement did convey the Commissioner's extreme dissatisfaction with rule 245.

These problems with the rule were not, however, of great moment, since the driver of the commuter train admitted at the inquiry that he did not have a detailed knowledge of rule 245 and suggested that there would be few people who did. The rule that he actually followed in the circumstances which confronted him that day was to stop and contact the signaller, ascertain the reason the light was red and then proceed in accordance with the instructions and the information provided. Drivers felt quite entitled to rely on signallers in this way because their training required them to "follow the instructions of the signaller". Moreover, if the signaller conveyed the information that the track ahead was clear, it made no sense to travel at walking speed, ready to stop at any obstruction; it was reasonable to travel at a speed which enabled the driver to stop at the next light, should it be red. That this was in fact the operating rule was confirmed by several other drivers who said that in the circumstances they would have behaved in the same way as the driver in question (McInerney, 2000a:48).

Where a violation of a formal safety rule is found to have contributed to an accident, there is an immediate tendency to blame the individual concerned in precisely the way that the commuter train driver was blamed for violating rule 245. It is clear from the preceding discussion that it would have been entirely inappropriate to blame the driver on this occasion. The safety literature provides a useful way of expressing this conclusion, known as the substitution test. The test is as follows. Mentally substitute the individual concerned with someone else who has the same training and experience and ask: "In the light of how events unfolded and were perceived by those involved ... is it likely that this new individual would have behaved any differently?" (Reason 1997:208). If the answer is no, then blame is inappropriate, for we are looking at a situation of systematic or patterned violation induced by the circumstances. The driver of the commuter train at Glenbrook passes the substitution test with flying colours, because other commuter train drivers would have behaved in the same way.

A culture of blame

The fact that the rules are so difficult to apply and that inspectors turn a blind eye to violations, raises the question of the real purpose of the rules. Several witnesses suggested that a major purpose was to ensure that someone could be punished when something went wrong. According to one: "I think a lot of the time [the rules] were added on to ensure punishment for the offender, not to make it any more safe" (McInerney, 2001:131).

The communication protocol was a case in point. Following earlier accidents in which the casual nature of the communication was seen to be a contributing factor, a communication protocol was set up specifying how communication was to occur. Nothing was done, however, to instruct people in the use of this protocol or to enforce its use. The inquiry described this as an "unconscionable failure" (McInerney, 2001:108). The view taken by employees was that the existence of the protocol enabled the rail authorities to blame accidents on the failure of employees to follow communication protocols and to resort to punishment as the appropriate response to an accident. One employee at the inquiry, when asked about the communication protocol, said he saw it simply as a "punishment tool".

This perception was supported by the Glenbrook inquiry itself, which looked at eight recent accident inquiries in the New South Wales rail system and found that each had focused on whether employees had violated safety rules and whether anyone deserved punishment. As the Commissioner put it:

> "I formed [the view] that the inquiries concentrated on which [rule] applied in the circumstances and whether the employees had been neglectful in choosing the correct one and properly applying it (McInerney, 2001:56)."

While the rules facilitate punishment, that can hardly be their purpose. There is something missing in this account. Another witness provided the missing link by suggesting that the purpose is "butt protection"; that is, the protection of the organisation. When an accident occurs and there is no rule which has been violated, the employer can be blamed for not foreseeing the possibility and doing something about it. Where there *is* a rule which has been violated, the employer can present itself as blameless because it has foreseen the accident and taken steps to forestall it. Blaming the violator is thus a by-product of a "butt protection" strategy, not an end in itself. This was an interpretation offered by the Commissioner himself: "you see, sometimes rules are made to protect the employer and if something happens they can say: why didn't you [obey the rule]?". On another occasion, he noted managers like to be able to refer to a rule which has been violated because, they believe, it "gets them out of hock". He went on to observe that this was a mistaken belief because under "the old common law system of negligence, the employer has to institute a safe system of work and not only that, must see that it is obeyed".

Further evidence of the punitive nature of the culture can be found in the behaviour of railway maintenance staff. When a driver reports a problem with a train, the matter is investigated by maintenance staff. Maintenance reports are supposed to be signed, presumably to ensure accountability, but drivers would occasionally go to the reports to see what response there had been to the problem and read "Nothing found", signed "FITTER". The fitters were clearly insisting on anonymity, lest they later be blamed and punished for having missed something.

The pervasive fear of punishment was recognised by one senior manager who said that when he joined State Rail Authority in 1998: "There was a degenerative culture ... in which people were scared of speaking up or reporting breaches because of fear of reprisal".

It needs to be pointed out the employees' fears of punishment were not unfounded. Two dramatic examples were provided to the inquiry. The first concerned a driver who reported a defective signal. When it was inspected by an electrician and found to be in good order, the driver was charged with making a mischievous report. This is a particularly tragic occurrence since safety in organisations is vitally dependent on the willingness of employees to report things which might be going wrong. The second example concerned a driver who refused to take a train out of the depot because water was dripping onto a dashboard near live wiring. The railways' response was to begin proceedings against him for refusing duty (McInerney, 2001:46).

There is important irony here. I have deliberately avoided talking about a culture of compliance because the rule-focused culture of the railways was not a culture of compliance. It was a culture of rule making and, when things went wrong, a culture which blamed people for violating the rules; in the normal course of events the authorities did very little to ensure compliance with the rules they had promulgated. The "unconscionable failure" to which the inquiry referred was a failure "to ensure compliance with the relevant protocol".

By contrast, one witness gave evidence of a culture of compliance which existed in the United Kingdom rail system in the early 1980s:

> "[There were] old fashioned sergeant major types of people who lived and breathed the rules and regulations, and were anxious to ensure that not only were people doing the right thing, but anxious to debate and would continuously create debate everywhere they went regarding the application of the rules in different environments, which rules would apply in testing people's knowledge ... [These sergeant major types] upheld the glory of very high operating standards ... and passed on the lessons of minor incidents as they went around ..."

This was in some respect a military regime, he said, because of the emphasis it placed on compliance. The metaphor is significant because it conveys a sense of the energy and resources which an organisation must devote in order to create a culture in which rules are obeyed. The witnesses noted that these sergeant major types no longer exist in the United Kingdom system, nor are they to be found in the New South Wales rail system.

The impact of rules on risk-awareness

There is a relationship between rules and risk. The railway safety rules have been developed as a response to risks revealed by accidents. The risk management process at the organisational level has identified a risk and set in place a rule as a means of controlling that risk. However, on a day-to-day basis there seemed to be little awareness of the risks which the rules were designed to control, and little attention paid to whether the rules were effective risk control measures.

The existence of rules seemed actually to deaden awareness of the risks which the rules were intended to control. The theory of accident prevention in complex and high risk systems is that there should be a series of measures in place to guard against each significant hazard. Accidents often occur when one of these protective systems is out of operation for some reason, and this is a time when people need to be especially sensitive to risk. Where a signal has failed to red and drivers are authorised to pass it, one of the regular safeguards against collision is not operating. This is a situation of heightened risk, where heightened awareness of risk would be desirable. The driver of the commuter train was not, however, sensitive to this heightened risk. His concern was whether or not he was authorised to pass, that is, with the rule as he understood it. When the signaller gave him this authorisation he assumed this meant the track was clear. The inquiry found that this was a reasonable assumption in the circumstances (McInerney, 2000a:49). Nevertheless, the driver knew that the *Indian Pacific* was somewhere ahead. He knew, too, that the *Indian Pacific* had stopped at the same signal a short while earlier. Had he been alert to the increased risks inherent in passing a red signal he could easily have asked the signaller where the *Indian Pacific* was. This might have led the signaller to realise that he had no idea where it was, which would in turn have led the driver to travel rather more cautiously.

Several other examples were provided to the inquiry of the way in which reliance on rules seemed to deaden risk-awareness. One of these is worth recounting. Track workers are obviously at risk of being hit by passing trains. Trains may be excluded from the particular track on which work is being done, but if they are using an adjacent track, travelling in the opposite direction, workers remain at considerable risk. In one accident a worker who was temporarily in the "six foot", the space between lines, was hit and killed by a train on the other line. It was obvious that workers might find themselves from time to time in the "six foot", but no precautions were put in place to protect them. The inquiry found that the safety rules applying in this situation were so complex that they distracted supervisors from applying any common sense (McInerney, 2001:86).

Finally, it has already been noted that investigations which are aimed at identifying rule violations tend to terminate at this point without going on to identify ways in which the job or the circumstances may have contributed to the accident. This is yet another way in which the focus on rules can deaden awareness of risk.

Conclusion

This chapter has highlighted the rule-focused nature of the railway culture. It was a culture in which a great deal of energy went into rule making, but very little into ensuring compliance. Indeed, had there been concerted effort to enforce the rules, their inadequacies would have become rapidly apparent. The real function of the rules was to demonstrate that the railway authorities had applied their minds to controlling risk and the rules seemed to be invoked primarily when things went wrong, in order to allocate blame, rather than in the normal course of events, to assure safety. In some respects the safety rules were antithetical to safety since they tended to deaden risk-awareness.

This analysis bears out one of the main contentions of Part A. In examining the relationship between culture and safety, it is not sufficient to ask to what extent the organisation in question exhibits a culture of safety. Rather, one must examine the culture of the organisation and then identify its impact on safety. One would have to conclude that the rule-making focus of the railway culture revealed in the Glenbrook inquiry was not conducive to safety and in fact contributed to a lack of risk-awareness.

Chapter 4
A culture of "silos"

This chapter deals with a second distinctive aspect of the railway culture revealed in the Glenbrook inquiry. There was a tendency to ignore problems facing people in other parts of the system and a failure to recognise that these problems might require a system-wide solution. Indeed, there was almost an antagonism between people carrying out different functions in the rail system. The situation was referred to during the inquiry as a "silo mentality", in which people retreat to their own organisational or occupational niches and deny any broader responsibilities. Job demarcation and the attitude that "it's not my job" are distinguishing features of the silo culture. Such a culture obviously compromises the goals of the larger organisation or system.

The Glenbrook inquiry revealed evidence of the silo mentality at two levels: first, at the level of the front line employees, in particular signallers and drivers; and second at the level of the organisations which employed them. The divisions between drivers and signallers were long standing, but the antagonism between the various rail organisations was a result of the fragmentation of the rail system which the Government had brought about in 1996. This chapter will look at these two levels in turn. It will show how the divisions which existed at both levels compromised safety.

The signaller in the Glenbrook crash

The role of the signaller in the Glenbrook train crash has so far remained unexamined in this book, but it was clearly crucial. Sitting in his signal box at Penrith, three stations on from Glenbrook, the signaller knew that the *Indian Pacific* was somewhere ahead of the commuter train, but he had no idea where. Nevertheless, he authorised the commuter train to proceed, in a manner which conveyed to the driver that the track was clear to the next signal. Here is the full conversation which took place between the signaller and driver:

> "Signaller: Yeah, 534?
>
> Driver: Yeah, who have I got there, matey?
>
> Signaller: Penrith, mate.
>
> Driver: Yeah, [the Glenbrook signal], I'm right to go past it, am I, mate?
>
> Signaller: Yeah, mate, you certainly are. Listen, can you get back to us? What was the previous signal showing?
>
> Driver: Yellow.

Signaller: Yellow, okay, and what's that signal exactly shown, just red or ... ?

Driver: Yeah, two reds, mate.

Signaller: Two reds, no worries. All right mate, can you just let us know what the signal in advance says when you get to it, thanks?

Driver: Okay, matey.

Signaller: Okay, thanks."

We do not need to understood the technicalities of this conversation here, but it should be obvious that the whole conversation is proceeding on the assumption that the red light is consequence of signal failure and that the signaller is seeking information about the impact of the failure on adjacent signals. His request to the driver to let him know the status of the next signal when he arrived there was taken by the driver to indicate that the line was unoccupied at least to the next signal and there is no doubt that the signaller assumed this to be the case.

Let us consider the situation which confronted the signaller. His primary motivation was to keep the trains running on time and he had little or no understanding of safety procedures (McInerney, 2000a:35). In particular, the signaller had no idea of the speed at which trains authorised to pass signals at red could be expected to travel. For him, the failed signal was simply an impediment to be worked around and did not represent a situation of increased risk. Apart from managing the failure of the signal, he was also pre-occupied with the fact that the *Indian Pacific* would shortly arrive at Penrith station. This was a complex, multi-platform station and the signaller would need to clear a path through the station. It was this which was uppermost in his mind at the time.

The *Indian Pacific* had stopped at the Glenbrook signal and had been delayed there for seven minutes before being authorised by the signaller to proceed. The very next signal was also red, for technical reasons related to the Glenbrook signal failure, and the *Indian Pacific* had stopped again, but this time the driver had been unable to contact the signaller because of difficulties with the trackside phone. The signaller seems to have assumed that because he had not heard from the *Indian Pacific* since it left the Glenbrook signal, it had encountered no further hold ups, and the line was therefore clear. In other words, in the absence of conclusive information to the contrary, the situation was assumed safe. Readers will recall that this was one of the elements of the culture of risk denial described in Part A. An expert witness at the inquiry pointed out that a signaller trained to be risk-aware would have presumed that the track was occupied until the contrary was established.

In authorising the commuter train driver to proceed, the signaller made no mention of the *Indian Pacific*. He did not tell him how long the *Indian Pacific* had been delayed at the Glenbrook signal, nor did he tell him that he was unaware of its location. He was not required by rule 245 to do so, and he apparently thought that these were not matters which needed to be passed on. Again, any employee who had been trained in risk awareness would have recognised that in this situation of heightened risk the driver should be provided with all available information. But the signaller displayed no such awareness. The report comments that this is part of a general pattern in which:

> "... important information concerning possible hazards or unusual conditions is not reported to train drivers. There is a prevailing attitude that train drivers should act in accordance with signal indications and receive no other assistance. That attitude does not show a collective approach which is so necessary for a safety culture (McInerney, 2001:46)."

Further evidence of the divisions between signallers and drivers

Although the existence of a silo mentality on the part of the signaller involved in the Glenbrook crash can be inferred from his behaviour, the evidence is indirect. The inquiry did, however, uncover much stronger evidence of this attitude. One of the eight other accident reports which the Glenbrook inquiry was asked to examine provided a dramatic example of the compartmentalised and antagonistic thinking which prevailed among signallers and drivers. A train controller had decided to divert a peak hour commuter train into a side loop at Hornsby station. He instructed a signaller to set the points and the signal accordingly and to alert the driver to what was happening, but the signaller failed to communicate with the driver as instructed. The driver was not expecting to be diverted and failed to see the diversion signal. As a result the train travelled at excessive speed into the side loop and ended up derailed. Subsequently, when signallers were asked to inform drivers in future of any unexpected route changes, they objected on the grounds that this was not their job and that it was the responsibility of drivers to recognise and respond to signals.

This attitude of non-cooperation must be seen in the context of a history of bad feeling between drivers and signallers. Evidence was given at the inquiry of a signaller who, from time to time, instructed drivers to behave in ways that violated procedures, presumably to keep trains running on time. So as to protect himself, the signaller chose on these occasions to communicate on phones or radios which had no recording facilities. On one such occasion, a driver who followed the signaller's instructions was punished for the violation, leading the union to impose a ban on receiving instructions other than in writing.

The Commissioner comments that "it is the duty of the trade unions to ensure that the safety of their members has the highest priority. It should be a priority above demarcation disputes" (McInerney, 2001:91). He does not come down heavily on unionism, however, because it is clear that blaming unions misses the organisational contribution to the problem.[1] Employees were not encouraged to think that they had any overall responsibility for rail safety; their function was simply to perform their particular job. The report notes that management discouraged drivers from questioning signals:

> "Apparently as a means of better ensuring on time running, drivers are discouraged from communicating with signallers to clarify the train movements that they are required to undertake (McInerney, 2001:93)."

Moreover, drivers, signallers and guards were traditionally trained in separate groups, which meant that they did not develop much understanding of the problems faced by the other groups. This further undermined cooperation. Another rail system mentioned at the inquiry places drivers into train controller jobs for six months at a time, which greatly improves the understanding in these two groups of problems facing the other. The absence of any such job rotation in the New South Wales system contributed to the occupational isolation and lack of trust which characterised the system.

The Hornsby accident described above involved a driver failing to see a signal. Misreading signals or failing to see red signals is a well-known cause of rail accidents, and several of the accidents investigated by the inquiry were of this nature. The railway term for failing to stop at a red light is "SPAD", or "signal passed at danger". It is symptomatic of the silo mentality of signallers that they see a SPAD as exclusively the driver's problem, in fact, the driver's fault. However, some signals are more SPAD-prone than others, immediately suggesting that there is something about the signal that is contributing to the problem. In the same year as the Glenbrook crash, a collision occurred at Ladbroke Grove in London, killing 31 people. The collision was a result of a SPAD, the ninth at this particular signal since it had been built in 1993. This was one of the most SPAD-prone signals in the whole of the United Kingdom — it was very difficult for drivers to see — yet signallers at Ladbroke Grove continued even after the accident to apportion blame to the drivers. The Ladbroke Grove accident report comments that this tendency of signallers to see SPADs as the responsibility of drivers alone is "a dangerously complacent attitude" (Cullen, 2001:3,55-56,94). Clearly, SPADing is best seen as a systemic problem requiring a systemic solution; a silo mentality undermines this approach.

---

1   The Commissioner was actually quite complimentary about the role played by the union in promoting safety (McInerney, 2001:164).

The impact of the disaggregation on employees

The disaggregation of the New South Wales rail system which occurred in 1996 increased the isolation of the occupational cultures described above. This is particularly apparent in the contraction of the role of stationmaster. In the previously integrated system, the stationmaster was a highly experienced rail employee who exercised a supervisory function over signallers in adjacent signal boxes and was familiar with the operations of their signal boxes. The stationmaster also had some responsibility for drivers passing through the station and was trained to assist drivers dealing with unusual situations. Disaggregation meant that, henceforth, stationmasters, signallers and drivers had less contact with one another. In particular, the stationmaster focused on providing customer service at stations and no longer had any role in the management of trains. This was relevant to the Glenbrook crash in the following way. The *Indian Pacific* had been held up at the Glenbrook station for seven minutes by the faulty signal. It had not long departed when the commuter train came to a halt at the Glenbrook station because of the same faulty signal. A stationmaster with some responsibility for train movements might have been alert to what was going on and spoken to the driver of the commuter train. In fact the stationmaster sat in his office and paid no attention to the unusual train behaviour at his station because he had no responsibility for what was happening. One of the recommendations made at the inquiry was that there should be additional station staff with authority to help trains through in unusual circumstances (McInerney, 2000b:25), and this very recommendation was a tacit admission of the consequences of disaggregation in this respect.

Disaggregation meant that signallers were no longer under the supervision of stationmasters, but it also left the signallers more isolated in another way. Prior to disaggregation, network control (which included signalling) had been a part of an integrated State Rail Authority. After disaggregation the network control function fell between two new organisational entities (see below), and signallers found themselves in something of a limbo. They were still visited by "superintendents", but these people failed to carry out any effective supervision with regard to safety rules and their prime function was to assist with on time running, as will be discussed in more detail in the next chapter.

The effect was that signallers felt themselves to be left out. As one said "we are the unseen operations part of the railway; out of sight, out of mind". This meant, as one signaller admitted, that they could get into "bad habits", such as failing to communicate information. One particular bad habit in the Penrith signal box was that signallers were accustomed to listening to commercial radio while doing their job, contrary to railway safety rules. One superintendent admitted at the inquiry that he was aware of this habit but did nothing about it (McInerney, 2000a:34).

It is clear, then, that the signaller whose behaviour contributed to the Glenbrook crash was part of an isolated occupational grouping which was not under effective supervision and had no particular awareness of safety issues or sense of responsibility for the way other parts of the system were functioning. This was an occupational silo, *par excellence*. The occupational isolation of the signallers was a longstanding aspect of railway culture, but it had been profoundly exacerbated by the fragmentation of the rail system into discrete commercial organisations in 1996.

Effect of disaggregation at organisational level

The disaggregation of the rail system was designed to promote competition and perhaps to pave the way for privatisation (although the latter has not occurred). According to the Commissioner:

> "... the changes in 1996 were driven more by ideological considerations based upon supposed competition theory than on how a very heavily patronised public utility could best be managed in the interests of efficiency and safety (McInerney, 2000b:11)."

Disaggregation involved splitting the previously integrated State Rail Authority into a number of entities, of which three are relevant here. The rail track and other infrastructure were vested in a Rail Access Corporation, the infrastructure *maintenance* section of the old Authority was set up as a second entity, known as Rail Services Australia, and the State Rail Authority itself was reconstituted as a passenger train operator.

Where did network control (signallers, train controllers, etc) fit into this new scheme? More than 90% of the trains travelling in the metropolitan area were local services run by the State Rail Authority (hereafter the SRA). There was an obvious argument, therefore, for giving network control to the SRA. Against this was the theoretical possibility that long-distance trains owned by other companies might get less favourable access to the rail network if network control was carried out by the metropolitan train operator. This latter argument won the day and the network control function was handed to the track owner, Rail Access Corporation, to ensure all train operators had equal access.

Although under the new arrangements the track owner also owned the network control infrastructure (signals etc), it had not been given the staff to operate it, so it engaged the network control section of the SRA to do the job on contract. The result was that a part of the SRA was no longer under the control of the SRA, but under the control of the track owner instead. An organisational wall had therefore to be put in place between network control staff and the remainder of the SRA, to ensure that the SRA did not unduly influence network controllers. This necessarily restricted communication. The report comments that this was "obviously an artificial and unsatisfactory state of affairs". The former chief executive officer of SRA provided the following illustration of the problem. SRA must run its trains in such a way as to meet passenger demand, yet under the new arrangements it was not in control of train timetables; that was a network control function. As a result of the communication restrictions which existed between the SRA and network control after disaggregation, the first train timetable to be introduced turned out to be unworkable (McInerney, 2000b:19).

The fragmentation of the rail system into distinct entities, each with its own agenda, created conflicts of interest where none had previously existed. Some of these conflicts had a direct impact on safety. For instance, the new rail entities refused to cooperate with safety audits which other entities wished to conduct. When the rail track owner wished to audit the wheels and the brakes of trains coming onto its track, train operators refused on the grounds that the rail track owner had no rights or responsibilities to do so. "No, that's not your job", they said. "Your job is to provide access" (McInerney, 2001:65).

Similarly, at one point the track owner became concerned about the performance of its contractor, the network control section of SRA. It decided to conduct an audit of employees in signal boxes, but the SRA refused it permission and said it would conduct its own audit. When this audit was completed, it refused to provide the results to the track owner. The judge was scathing in his condemnation of the SRA. "So much for cooperation between the various entities on safety critical issues", he said. "This culture of secrecy and lack of accountability by one organisation to another must cease" (McInerney, 2001:147,148). It is clear that the silo mentality of the new rail entities was every bit as problematic as that which existed at the employee level.

The Commissioner found that all eight recent accidents he had been asked to consider had been "inevitably produced" by disaggregation (McInerney, 2001:36). One example will suffice. A piece of track built in the late 1990s to service Sydney's new Olympic Park had unusually tight curvature at one point. This meant that there would be high sideways forces on train wheels at this point, which would cause abrasion and rapid wheel wear. The designers therefore specified that special lubricants be applied to the track to overcome the problem. However, the 2000 Olympic Games were to be "green" games, and the Olympic Coordination Authority vetoed the use of lubricants. The track owner, not being responsible for the condition of rolling stock, accepted this veto without attempting to find environmentally acceptable alternatives (which were in fact available). The predictable wheel wear occurred and finally resulted in a derailment. In an integrated rail organisation, the interaction of track and wheels would be handled in an integrated way. But in the fragmented rail system, the physical wheel/rail interface coincided with the interface of two distinct organisations, each with different goals. Lack of adequate coordination at organisational interfaces is a well-known safety risk,[2] and the Olympic Park derailment was a classic example of the problem.

The commercial imperative

The track owner, Rail Access Corporation, and the track maintainer, Rail Services Australia, were both set up under the new arrangements as corporations, to be run on commercial lines. I shall show in this section that this made cooperation between the three entities even more difficult. Rail Access Corporation had inherited the rail infrastructure with a requirement that it be maintained at least in its 1996 condition. From a commercial point of view it made no sense for Rail Access Corporation to upgrade or improve the asset. Moreover, it had no obligation to passengers to do so, as the following interchange made clear:

> "Q: If you don't provide a track which is sufficient for meeting the needs of SRA's train services to transport their passengers about, there is no penalty provision at present?
>
> A: That's correct.
>
> Q: There's no sanction whatsoever?
>
> A: Correct."

On the other hand, the SRA needed to satisfy passenger demand and provide a punctual and reliable service. It therefore needed improvements in track and signalling as its operations developed, and it found itself in the anomalous position of having to pay the track owner to improve its own asset, in addition to paying an annual fee for access to the track. The Commissioner was aghast at hearing this, describing the situation as one of "chaos and confusion". Even a request from the SRA for a new signal or for the movement of an existing one could be met with resistance from the track owner. An executive from the track owning company told the inquiry:

> "When we receive those requests they are normally outside our current plans and yes, they provide a drain on the work and the resources that we had planned to apply to the infrastructure during that period."

Not only did the new arrangements tend to impede improvements in the rail infrastructure, but they also led, over time, to an unacceptable level of infrastructure failure. In the month of January 2000 there were 35 train delays caused by infrastructure failure, in which 11,000 passengers experienced an average delay of 15 minutes. It was just such a failure, the failure of the Glenbrook signal, which initiated the Glenbrook accident sequence.

---

2   For another example, see the Ararat train crash in which four organisations were responsible for control of the points, which meant in practice that none exercised effective control (ATSB, 2000).

Maintenance was not actually done by the track owner, Rail Access Corporation; the work was subcontracted to Rail Services Australia. But the track owner was not in a position to control its contractor effectively, because disaggregation meant that the expertise in rail network maintenance lay with the contractor, not the track owner. Moreover, it could not be presumed that the track maintainer would use this expertise in the best interests of the New South Wales railways, because it, too, had been set up as a commercial enterprise and pursued its commercial objectives by looking for work outside of New South Wales. In four years it had won maintenance contracts in most Australian States and in Hong Kong. The chief executive officer of the track maintenance company was asked at the inquiry whether this meant "that the resources of the company were spread a little too thinly and were not therefore adequate for the proper maintenance of the New South Wales system". He denied this suggestion, but he did concede that in the light of the level of infrastructure failure, the level of maintenance being done was inadequate.

The view that the resources of the company were spread too thinly was supported by an influential expert witness who told the inquiry:

> "I don't believe it is in the best interests of this system to do other than have its expert maintainer concentrating on the maintenance of this system...This system should be the first priority."

The Commissioner accepted this view and recommended that the rail maintenance organisation be re-amalgamated with the rail owner.

Just prior to the 2000 Sydney Olympic Games the Government appointed a Coordinator-General of Rail to provide direction for the whole rail system. This man told the inquiry his purposes were:

> "Firstly, to coordinate the activities of the three authorities and secondly, to look at their preparation for the Olympics in particular and to address some of the reliability issues that had become apparent over the previous twelve months."

In appointing a Coordinator-General of Rail, the Government was formally recognising that disaggregation had thrown the rail system into chaos, by creating a "cultural rift", to use the Commissioner's term (McInerney, 2001:48). The Government was constrained to act because the 2000 Olympics would put Sydney under the spotlight and a dysfunctional rail system at this time would be intolerable.

Disaggregation had replaced a single organisation focused on delivering a reliable rail service with three organisations pursuing different agendas and distrustful of, and antagonistic to, one another. Only the SRA was focused on delivering a reliable passenger service; the other two were driven by a commercial imperative which was not consistent with the interests of passengers. Moreover, the inquiry found that safety was one of the losers in this chaotic system:

> "The Glenbrook rail accident and the other [eight] rail accidents ... together illustrate the way in which disaggregation has been unsuccessful and has created an inefficient and unsafe rail network (McInerney, 2000b:27)."

Conclusion

This chapter set out to describe an aspect of the New South Wales rail culture which contributed to the Glenbrook accident — a tendency towards compartmentalisation. The various occupational groups displayed uncooperative, even antagonistic, attitudes towards one another, and one group, the signallers, seemed particularly cut off from other parts of the rail system. Communication between these groups was limited and relatively unhelpful, and the signaller's failure to provide the commuter train driver with safety-critical information was one of the central causes of the Glenbrook accident.

The silo mentality evident among front line employees was even more striking at the organisational level. The various rail organisations were pursuing different agendas and at times refused to cooperate with one another.

This was detrimental to safety in a variety of ways.

It should be noted, too, that the divisions which existed at the organisational level tended to reinforce the divisions which existed at the front line. Signallers worked for network control and local train drivers for the SRA; separating network control from the SRA could only widen the gap between signallers and drivers.

I have described all this as a culture of silos. It was a culture given to secrecy, non-cooperation, restricted communication and antagonism between occupational groups and organisations. It was a culture in which problems which were best seen as systemic were instead viewed as the exclusive concern of one group or another. The railways are not unique in this respect. Many organisations function in compartmentalised ways, but the New South Wales railway system was perhaps an extreme case, to which the policy of disaggregation had contributed in no small measure.

Chapter 5
On time running

One of the most striking aspects of the railway culture revealed in the Glenbrook inquiry was its emphasis on punctuality, or "on time running". The inquiry was told by people at all levels in the organisational hierarchy, from chief executive to driver, that "on time running is king", "on time running is everything" and "on time running is the holy grail" (McInerney, 2001:12,13). The Commissioner formed the view that this attitude had compromised safety:

> "It had become so entrenched in the attitudes of railway operational personnel that they could no longer objectively assess anomalous situations. They had developed an attitude that could not be varied under any circumstances — trains had to run on time despite the consequences (McInerney, 2001:42-43)."

The conflict between on time running and safety is the railway version of the well-known conflict between production and safety. In many organisations, the importance of production is emphasised daily to employees with the result that it takes priority over safety in subtle and not so subtle ways. Moreover, this occurs despite stated policies that put safety first. In the railway context there is a similar publicly stated commitment to putting safety first which is nevertheless compromised by the overwhelming culture of on time running. At one point in the proceedings, the Commissioner became so exasperated with the safety first rhetoric that, when a witness explained yet again that the priorities were "safety first and then, on time running", he responded, "I have heard about that ad nauseam".

Some evidence of just how the culture of on time running interfered with safety will be provided later in this chapter. But the aim of the chapter is not primarily to demonstrate the impact of on time running on safety. It is to examine the culture of on time running itself, whence it came and how it was maintained. For this was a remarkably powerful and effective aspect of railway culture, and examining it may provide insights into how a powerful and effective culture of safety might be developed.

The source of the culture of on time running

The culture of on time running originates *outside* the railways. As the Commissioner noted:

> "The travelling public and the media appear to judge the SRA [State Rail Authority] principally on whether or not its trains are running on time. It is understandable that the public regards it as important that the trains run on time. Every day over the radio the daily performance of the rail network in regards to the punctuality of trains is frequently broadcast (McInerney, 2001:42)."

The report goes on:

> "As with all organisations, railway employees do not live isolated from the society of which they are a part. Consequently, they are influenced by any public scrutiny of their actions and their employer. There is little doubt that the continuing criticism of the SRA for failing to ensure trains ran on time, had a filter down effect through the ranks of the SRA. Consequently, individual employees, no matter what their function, had a significantly heightened awareness of the importance of on time running."

These are important observations. It is clear that the culture of an organisation will be powerfully shaped by the needs of external stakeholders such as passengers or, in other contexts, shareholders. Where stakeholder interest is championed by the press and politicians, as it is in the case of railway commuters, it becomes an irresistible force moulding the organisational culture.

The practices of the culture of on time running

As noted in Part A, a culture is not just a mindset; it is also a set of practices. Let us consider the practices associated with the culture of on time running. The most striking practices were the very close monitoring of the extent to which trains ran on time and the energetic response to any delays detected. The target the SRA aimed for was to have all trains arriving at their destinations within three minutes of the scheduled time. Train controllers entered a report on any late arrivals at Sydney terminal. If the reason for the delay was not obvious, an inspector would interview the driver. According to one driver, the tone of such an interview could be quite intimidating: "You lost time, son. Where? Speak up, speak clearly." If the reason provided to the inspector was unsatisfactory, a more senior manager may have spoken to the driver. In extreme cases, the driver might have been issued with a formal warning, or fined or suspended for a day (McInerney, 2001:13). From time to time reports were circulated to drivers showing the percentage of trains arriving on time. These practices ensured that the need to be on time remained at the forefront of every driver's mind.

Although only summary on time running reports were circulated to drivers, the statistics were calculated in such a way that senior managers had a very detailed and up to the minute idea of how well their system was performing in this respect. The figures were assembled twice daily so that performances during each morning and evening peak times could be separately assessed. The manager for network operations told the inquiry that indeed he examined the figures twice daily. By way of contrast, the only safety statistics he saw were the numbers of injuries occurring to train crews and signallers, and these were made available to him once a fortnight. In short, management had set up a system which enabled it to monitor performance with respect to on time running in an extraordinarily detailed way. The point was made in Part A that leaders create cultures by what they systematically pay attention to. It is clear that the culture of on time running was created in just this way.

But it was not just drivers who felt the pressure of on time running; so, too, did train controllers. A board is located in the vicinity of the office of the controllers indicating the percentage of on time running in the area that they control. One controller acknowledged that on time running was a constant pressure in the job and in the forefront of his mind at all times. The main part of his job, as he saw it, was to ensure that trains are on time. Controllers plot the progress of trains under their control and know at all times just how close to schedule they are. Thus it was that the controller monitoring the progress of the commuter train involved in the Glenbrook accident knew that it was three minutes late at Springwood, a few stations before Glenbrook. He knew, too, that it had been between two and three minutes late at earlier stations. The full significance of this will become apparent later; I mention it here simply to provide an indication of just how closely controllers monitored the situation.

Controllers tracked trains by speaking to signallers along the route and the language used for this communication is telling. Shortly before the crash, the signaller at Springwood conveyed to the controller that the commuter train, train 534, arrived at Springwood platform at 8.04 and departed at 8.05. What he actually said was: "534 was 4, 5." This is a highly condensed piece of communication which relies on a great deal of context for its meaning. The context is that both parties know that what is of interest is the time to the minute when the train arrived at and left the station and that this would have occurred at a few minutes past eight o'clock. What is of crucial concern is just how many minutes past eight. Given the extent of the common understanding which existed between these two men, the expression "534 was 4, 5" was enough to convey the necessary information. This style of shorthand communication can only occur where practices are routine and everyone is clear about the type of information which is to be communicated. In short, it can only occur where there is a well-developed understanding of "the way we do things around here" — a well-developed culture. The existence of this shorthand is testimony to the strength of the culture of on time running.

Signallers, too, were under pressure to ensure on time running. They were visited from time to time by so-called "network operations superintendents". These people did not understand the operations of the signals boxes and were not in a position to provide supervision to signallers. Nor were they in a position to assist with questions of safety. Their function was purely to monitor peak hour running to ensure that signallers were doing their bit to keep trains running on time. They had a disciplinary role in this respect for they were in a position to issue formal warnings to signallers who delayed trains unnecessarily. The Commissioner commented on this situation as follows:

> "The so-called superintendents did not superintend anything except on time running. It is therefore not surprising that at the forefront of the minds of the employees responsible for managing trains through this automatic section of track with at least one failed signal was the motivation to keep the trains moving through the section of track with little or no understanding or regard for the procedures (McInerney, 2000a:35)."

On time running and the Glenbrook accident

The circumstances surrounding the Glenbrook accident provide a glimpse of this culture of on time running in action. As noted above, the controller who was following the progress of the ill-fated commuter train was aware that it was running a couple of minutes behind schedule. He was aware, too, that the *Indian Pacific* had previously stopped for a full seven minutes at the Glenbrook station because of the failed signal. The reasons for this extended delay will be discussed later. A seven-minute delay for a commuter train which was already two minutes behind schedule would be a matter of great concern. These were the circumstances in which the controller got on the phone to the commuter train driver and told him that the Glenbrook signal which lay ahead was reported to have failed. The driver told the controller he would contact the signaller when he arrived at Glenbrook, meaning that he would stop and seek authorisation to proceed. The controller then said to the driver:

> "Well, yeah, it's only an auto so just trip past it."

This is a crucial comment, the meaning of which was subject to much debate at the inquiry. What was the controller trying to convey to the driver?

Consider the first part of the statement: "it's only an auto". Was this intended to downgrade the significance of the signal? The controller denied it, but in the circumstances, no other conclusion was possible. Automatic signals are designed to prevent trains which are running one behind another on the same piece of track from getting too close to each other. Where tracks cross, or there are points involved, non-automatic signals will be used; that is, signals set by signallers. The general perception was that a signal protecting a crossover or points was more important than an automatic signal on a single piece of track.

Consider, now, the second part of the statement: "just trip past it". If there is a trip mechanism on a signal, and a trip device on a train, then, if a train approaches a red signal at speed, the brakes will be applied automatically, bringing it to a standstill. If the train is travelling sufficiently slowly, the trip mechanism will not come into operation. Where signals and trains were equipped with trip mechanisms, and where the driver could see that the track ahead was clear, rule 245 allowed trains to proceed slowly past an automatic signal at red, without coming to a full stop, and *without contacting the signaller*. A train which passed a signal in this way would be said to be "tripping past the signal".

The Glenbrook signal was *not* fitted with a trip device, so the idea of "tripping past the signal" made no sense, strictly speaking. How, then, was this instruction to be understood? The commuter train driver understood the controller to be telling him to proceed past the signal without coming to a dead standstill and without contacting the signaller, *as if* both train and signal were equipped with trip mechanisms. "He was telling me to just go past that stick at stop, really, without contacting anyone."

The controller disputed this interpretation but the Commissioner accepted it and found that the controller had in effect been telling the driver to go past the signal without contacting the signaller. He found that the controller's motive was to ensure that the commuter train would not be held up at the Glenbrook signal in the way that the *Indian Pacific* had been (McInerney, 2000a:45,46).

Here, then, is a dramatic example of the culture of on time running in operation. It is an episode in which we see just how closely train controllers monitor on time running and how they see their job as intervening in order to minimise delays. We see too that the intervention was understood by the driver as a pressure to bend the rules in order to minimise delays.

It should be observed that the controller did not believe he was compromising safety in any way. He believed that the track ahead of the Glenbrook signal was clear and he may not even have been aware that he was asking the driver to violate the letter of the law. This person was just as blind to the risks inherent in the situation as the signaller was, and was single-mindedly focused on keeping the commuter train as close to schedule as possible. The driver, however, had no intention of accepting the advice of the controller and, as we know, stopped at Glenbrook and contacted the signaller. In so doing, he was resisting the pressure to achieve on time running no matter what the cost.

The *Indian Pacific*

The experience of interstate trains in the Sydney area provides further evidence of the significance of on time running. The pressure to run on time, that is, within three minutes of schedule, applied particularly to commuter trains. That kind of punctuality was far less important for interstate travellers. Many of the passengers on the *Indian Pacific*, for example, were tourists on holidays, and to them arriving in Sydney half an hour late after a long journey would not have seemed a matter of great moment. Interstate train drivers were, therefore, not as concerned as local commuter train drivers to run on time, and their behaviour differed accordingly.

The *Indian Pacific* had spent seven minutes at the Glenbrook signal before setting off. The driver had had difficulty getting through to the signaller, but persisted, and finally received authorisation to proceed. The signaller was critical of this long delay:

> "I didn't know why he was there for five minutes. Being only an auto, I thought if he couldn't establish contact with me then he would have proceeded after one minute. Five minutes just seemed like a long time, that all."

This is an interesting comment. It is true that the rules allowed the driver to move off after one minute if he could not contact the signaller. A driver focused on on time running might have been expected to do just that. But the *Indian Pacific* driver was willing to persist in his attempts to contact the signaller, in order to get a more definitive outcome. His behaviour had caused consternation to both the train controller and the signaller, who described the situation as involving "a bloody stack of dramas".

After passing the Glenbrook signal, the driver of the *Indian Pacific* continued to behave in ways that the signaller did not expect. He proceeded with extreme caution, at a speed which never exceeded 18 kilometres per hour. The signaller had no idea the *Indian Pacific* would travel so slowly, and for this reason he assumed that it was already well clear of the area when he authorised the commuter train to proceed.

Sociologists have often noted that the best way to establish what the implicit rules are in any social situation is to violate them and observe what happens (Garfinkel, 1967). That proposition is well illustrated here: the reaction of the signaller and the controller to the *Indian Pacific's* violations of the implicit rules about on time running is the clearest evidence of the existence of those rules.

The safety manager for the National Rail Corporation, the operator of the *Indian Pacific*, was quite explicit about this at the inquiry. He confirmed that his trains complied strictly with the rule about travelling with extreme caution after passing signals at stop, and he gave evidence that his drivers were criticised for so doing:

"Our drivers are criticised by the signaller in terms of the amount of time it has taken for us to work through that section having passed through signals at stop. We regularly get criticised for having lost time because we are blocking CityRail services."

Just as a current of water is most obvious when it encounters obstacles in its path, so the culture of on time running was most apparent when it encountered the resistance of an organisation like National Rail.

The conflict between on time running and safety

The aim of this chapter, so far, has been to demonstrate the power of the culture of on time running. Such a culture is not necessarily detrimental to safety. But in the absence of any countervailing culture of risk-awareness, the culture of on time running indeed undermined safety.

It contributed to the Glenbrook accident in the following way. The controller had encouraged the commuter train driver to pass the Glenbrook signal without contacting the signaller. This intervention did not have the intended effect, but it did influence the driver in another way. It conveyed to him that the track ahead of the signal was clear (McInerney, 2000a:46). So, when he eventually spoke to the signaller, his words were: "I'm right to go past it, am I, mate?" The signaller's response confirmed his presumption. This presumption in turn affected the driver's speed after he left the Glenbrook signal. In short, the controller's intervention, motivated by a desire to keep the train running on time, contributed indirectly to the Glenbrook crash.

Various other instances in which safety was sacrificed to punctuality came to light at the inquiry and are worth mentioning here. In one of the additional accidents considered by the inquiry, a train had passed a signal at stop and subsequently derailed. The signal was protected by a trip mechanism which was designed automatically to stop the train if it was approaching the stop signal at too great a speed. The speed at which the trip is intended to operate is specified in the safety rules as 25 kilometres per hour or above. The speed trigger had, however, been raised by unknown persons to 35 kilometres per hour, the only possible reason being to enable trains to travel faster on this section of the track. Had the trigger been set at 25 kilometres per hour, as it should have been, the derailment would not have occurred. The Commissioner commented as follows:

"An apparent desire to increase the speed at which trains pass intermediate train stops seems consistent to me with only one view, namely that safety is compromised for the purposes of increasing the speed at which trains move, an imperative of on time running (McInerney, 2001:103)."

Drivers were also under pressure to operate trains which were known before they left the depot to be defective. At times they were forced to drive trains with non-functioning radios and at times they were expected to drive trains with defective brakes. Drivers are told that unless they agree, perhaps a thousand people will be left stranded at stations. On one such occasion it was only because the union stepped in that management accepted that a train could not be driven in the condition it was in. As the witness said: "I can't emphasise [enough] the immense pressure being applied in pursuit of on time running here."

Finally, evidence was given at the inquiry of some specific circumstances which encourage drivers to speed. The timetable may specify a "dwell time" at a station of 40 seconds, say, which turns out to be quite unrealistic. Drivers then have to speed to make up lost time. Again, where the track has decayed due to the lack of adequate maintenance, the response is to put speed restrictions on the affected sections of track, which makes it even harder to maintain on time running without speeding elsewhere.

On time running in the United Kingdom

The inquiry into the Ladbroke Grove crash in 1999 in London revealed a similar focus on on time running. If anything, the focus was even greater than in New South Wales. One practice which maintained the culture in the United Kingdom was the requirement imposed on drivers that they provide written reports explaining any deviation from timetables. Drivers found this particularly burdensome and it contributed to what they perceived as an intolerable pressure to run on time. The pressure was backed by the threat of dismissal in extreme cases (Cullen, 2001:69).

As noted earlier, the culture of on time running stems from pressures lying outside rail organisations, specifically from the pressure of public opinion. In the United Kingdom, this external public pressure was reinforced by the possibility of fines imposed on offending companies. The Ladbroke Grove inquiry chair made the following observation:

"When I consider these views along with, in particular, the mechanisms for the imposition of penalties for poor performance [with respect to punctuality], in consequence of which fines of millions of pounds may be imposed by the Rail Regulator, and contrast these penalties, actual and potential, against the level of fines imposed in criminal proceedings in respect of serious breaches of health and safety, I concluded that the magnitude of the penalties that are likely to be imposed for poor performance, and the gross disparity which exists between performance and safety sanctions respectively, may well have conveyed to the industry the message that performance was the top priority (Cullen, 2001:42)."

The existence of this kind of external regulatory pressure made the pressure to sacrifice safety to on time running even greater in the United Kingdom than in New South Wales.

Conclusion

On time running in the New South Wales rail system was not just a mindset created by public demand for punctuality. It consisted of a set of practices which involved people at all levels. These practices included detailed performance monitoring and sanctions of various sorts against those who failed to comply. It involved a massive organisational effort, with large numbers of people whose sole job was to ensure that trains ran on time, and it expressed itself in the very language they used. All this involved a considerable commitment of resources. Clearly, organisations that want things to happen must devote the resources necessary to make them happen. Finally, it involved not just the stated commitment of leaders but their active and systematic attention; it was they who set up the organisational structures and practices to create the culture of on time running. The culture existed because they had created it.

On time running was a powerful aspect of the railway culture. I have chosen to analyse it here, not as a negative phenomenon — the enemy of safety — but as a cultural phenomenon of interest in its own right. The analysis shows how cultures are developed and maintained. On time running occupies the same pre-eminent position in the railway context that production occupies in many other industrial contexts. Analysing how companies keep the focus on production would reveal a comparable organisational effort.

The implications for safety are clear. A culture of safety requires a similar organisational effort. It is not a question of haranguing people to develop the appropriate mindset. Rather, leaders must develop organisational structures and practices which encourage and reward risk-awareness.

In the absence of a countervailing culture of safety, a culture of on time running, or any equivalent culture of production, can be expected to undermine safety in a quite systematic and predictable way. On the other hand, a powerful culture of safety is not necessarily at the expense of other organisational goals. Given the right organisational practices and incentives, people can focus on a primary organisational goal and at the same time remain risk-aware. Nevertheless, there will be times when these two imperatives collide and it will be the behaviour of leaders at these times which determines the outcome.

There is one other lesson which emerges from this discussion. The culture of on time running derives its strength from outside the rail organisations, from public pressure, and, in the United Kingdom, from the threat of penalties imposed by the regulator in the event of delays. An equivalently powerful culture of safety may depend on similar external pressures. Public opinion becomes a powerful force when major accidents occur, but because train crashes are relatively rare, public opinion cannot provide the constant external pressure which appears to be necessary to create a powerful performance culture. Perhaps it will only be when safety regulators wield as big a stick as the on time performance regulator does in the United Kingdom that we can expect a similarly powerful culture of safety.

Chapter 6
A risk-blind culture

To be *blind* to risk means to be unaware of it. To *deny* risk implies some degree of awareness or risk, coupled with a more active rejection of its significance.[1] Was the railway culture at the time of the Glenbrook crash merely risk-blind, or was it more actively risk-denying?

Various examples were provided to the inquiry in which drivers brought hazards to the attention of supervisors only to have their concerns dismissed. As noted earlier, they were expected to take trains out with defective radios, speedometers and even brakes. A union representative told the inquiry of a situation in which the brakes of newly imported wagons had proved incapable of holding a train on a steep section of track. The union had had to place bans on the trains until the braking system was changed (McInerney, 2001:164). The resistance which drivers encountered implies an active denial of the significance of risks to which they had drawn attention. As the inquiry was told, "risk-denial by workers, supervisors and managers when confronted with degraded operations" was widespread.

In many other situations, however, the evidence provided to the inquiry revealed only a lack of risk-awareness, rather than a more active denial of risk. For example, the signaller who authorised the commuter train to go pass the Glenbrook signal at red had not considered and then rejected the possibility that the *Indian Pacific* might be in the way. Had he done so it would be appropriate to describe his state of mind as one of risk-denial. The fact is that the risk of collision had not even entered his mind; he was simply lacking in any awareness of that risk.

Clearly, the distinction between being unaware of risk and denying it is a fine one. If the driver of the commuter train had asked the signaller where the *Indian Pacific* was, thereby implicitly raising the safety issue, it is quite possible that the signaller would have replied that he was expecting it at any moment to arrive at Penrith station. Such a response would have amounted to a denial of the risk of collision. In short, particular circumstances may transform risk-blindness into risk-denial. Much of the risk-blindness evident in the inquiry may well have turned to more active risk-denial, had the subject of risk ever

---

1   Dr Sally Leivesley (2000:3) provided the following definition to the inquiry: *Risk Denial* is a denial of the likelihood that factors in the environment will create consequences despite those factors being perceived and the risk being foreseeable. *Risk Unaware* or *Non-Awareness of Risk* describes a state of lack of consciousness or knowledge of risk.

been raised. But it seems that it wasn't. For that reason, the organisational culture will be described here as one of risk-blindness, rather than risk-denial.

There is a second preliminary matter to be addressed here. I defined culture earlier as a set of practices. Denial is an active process and a culture of risk-denial presumes a set of associated practices. However, there are no specific practices associated with a culture of risk-blindness. Such a culture is simply one in which the practices of risk-awareness are absent. In what follows, therefore, the discussion will necessarily be about the behaviours which would have been expected in a culture of risk-awareness and a demonstration of how these were missing from the New South Wales rail system at the time of the Glenbrook crash.

The context

The lack of risk-awareness started at the very top — with government. The disaggregation of the rail system in 1996 could be expected to introduce a host of new risks into the system, arising from the way the new rail entities interacted or failed to interact with one another. But the New South Wales Government did not recognise this possibility and assumed that the safety arrangements of the existing system could be transferred, unaltered, to the new regime (McInerney, 2001:72). By way of contrast, prior to the rail disaggregation which took place in the United Kingdom in 1994, the government required a so-called "dispositional" statement to be prepared. The aim was to show that all safety responsibilities in the existing structure would be located with one or other entity in the disaggregated structure, and that there were no gaps or overlaps. Overlaps, it was thought, would be just as problematic as gaps, since they would generate confusion about who was actually responsible. Disaggregation is a particular form of organisational change and it is well recognised that significant organisational changes need to be risk-assessed. The United Kingdom Government was aware of this principle; the New South Wales Government was not.

The new rail entities took their lead from government. A list of hazards,[2] claimed to be a complete list, had been drawn up by the rail authority in 1989. At the time of disaggregation this list was simply taken over by the new entities without review and without any consideration of whether disaggregation had introduced any further risks. Moreover, there had been no attempt to update the controls specified for dealing with these hazards by the time of the Glenbrook crash. In short, it was a static document that had not moved with the times and could be presumed to have declined in relevance. The Commissioner concluded: "I have the clear impression that over time this hazard list has not been used as a risk management process to manage safety,

---

2   In some contexts the distinction between hazard and risk is an important one. The distinction
     is not vital in the present discussion and the terms will be used interchangeably here.

but rather as a means to deflect any criticism from the rail organisation concerned when an accident or incident occurred" (McInerney, 2001:72).

The concept of a complete hazard list is, in any case, problematic. It assumes a finite and relatively small number of ways in which things can go wrong. In reality there are innumerable ways things can go wrong; in particular, there are innumerable ways in which controls that are supposed to be in place to deal with a recognised hazard can fail. Major accident investigations frequently reveal that the accident was not the consequence of some unrecognised hazard. On the contrary, the hazard had been identified and controls put in place, but for some reason the controls were not effective, perhaps because they had been tampered with, perhaps because they had not been maintained, perhaps because they had been phased out or downgraded as a cost-cutting measure. One witness at the inquiry called these control failures second-level hazards. A collision between two trains travelling in the same direction is a principal hazard which is supposed to be controlled by automatic signals and special procedures to be implemented when such signals fail. Yet as the Glenbrook crash shows, the controls themselves can fail, in ways that introduce further hazards into the system. This is overlooked by the railway presumption that it can list and therefore control all hazards.

Finally, it should be noted here that following disaggregation the rail organisations made no effort to consider how their own activities might impact on other organisations in the rail network. For instance, the rail track owner, which also owned the signals, did not recognise that signal failure might contribute to accidents and that it was therefore incumbent on the infrastructure owner to drive the failure rate of signals down as close to zero as possible. Its view was that, provided drivers complied scrupulously with rule 245, signal failure was not a risky event. This view failed to recognise that signal failure puts stress on the entire rail system and that accidents are more likely in these circumstances. There have indeed been fatal accidents after drivers dutifully stopped at failed signals and then proceeded in accordance with various special rules.

It is interesting that one executive who joined the railways in 1998 from another industry, highlighted this very point:

> "I challenged the steering group that really if we were to lead safety we shouldn't have a procedure for passing signals that have failed. All stop signals should be absolute. That is, if a signal is at red, the train doesn't proceed. What I am challenging there is the paradigm of unreliability of those signals. [I advocate] methods by which you make them more reliable, so a train can proceed with the full benefit of the signalling system."

Another witness summed it up as follows:

> "Anything you do which undermines the sanctity of a red light ... is not a good thing to do in railway safety."

But the mistakes which drivers might make after being authorised to proceed through a red light were not the responsibility of the rail track owner in a disaggregated system. Such risks were therefore ignored when it came to spending money on signal reliability.

The failure to risk-assess the communications technology

One of the factors which contributed quite specifically to the Glenbrook accident was the technology in use for communication between drivers, signallers and controllers. There were no fewer than five different communication systems involved in the accident. The commuter train was equipped with a Sydney-area two-way radio which enabled it to communicate with the signaller and the controller, but not the driver of any other train. The *Indian Pacific* was equipped with a second two-way radio system which enabled it to communicate with drivers of other long-distance trains, as well as signallers. A third radio system was also available to the drivers of the *Indian Pacific*, the signaller and the guard on the commuter train, but not the commuter train driver or the train controller. Mobile phones were available to some railway staff. Finally, there were phones at the base of each signal which enabled drivers to communicate with signallers. This latter system was antiquated technology which required the driver to get down from the train, walk to the phone box, open it with a key (if it was locked) and crank a handle fifteen times in order to get the attention of the signaller at the other end.

The Commissioner was incredulous at the antiquated nature of this system:

> "Perhaps he could send up a smoke signal. Really, in the 21st century, a technology that was early 20th century is still being used to communicate. I find that very difficult to understand."

Drivers of commuter trains who were seeking permission to pass signals at stop could use the local Sydney-area radio, but drivers of interstate trains were required to communicate with signallers using the phone on the signal post. So, when the *Indian Pacific* arrived at the Glenbrook signal, the driver had to get down from his train and walk across to the signal phone box. These boxes were not normally locked, so he did not have his key with him. On this occasion it was inexplicably locked and he had to walk back to his train to get the key. This is why the *Indian Pacific* experienced a seven-minute delay before obtaining authorisation and moving off again, and it was this delay which had caused the signaller and controller such concern (McInerney, 2000a:40).

Arriving at the next signal, which was also at stop, the driver again alighted and tried to contact the signaller by cranking the handle on the phone. On this occasion he failed to get through to the signaller, perhaps because the signaller was talking to someone else (McInerney, 2000a:52), and he finally decided to move off without specific authorisation. He had been delayed at this second signal another three minutes and had just started to move when the commuter train crashed into his rear.

Had the *Indian Pacific* been allowed to communicate with the signaller using its two-way radio system, communication would have been far more efficient and the accident would have been averted. Instead, the driver was required to use a method which was, as the Commissioner found, "time wasting and inefficient and undoubtedly contributed to the accident" (McInerney, 2000a:69).

The multiplicity of communication systems in itself poses risks. As one expert witness put it:

> "The inability of the front-line operators to talk to each other through common methods, or to be able to make contact with each other is, at best, a breakdown, and at worst a total failure in assessment of any risks."

But the use of the antiquated signal phone system involved a more specific set of risks. To require an interstate passenger train which is moving through the suburban network at peak hour to use such a time-wasting technology in the event of signal breakdown can be expected to put particular stresses on the system. We know, moreover, that the risks are higher when a system is under stress in this way. Yet these risks were not even recognised, let alone assessed or managed.

Putting all this another way, the railway timetable is a "tightly coupled" system, in the sense that disturbances in any part of the system can be expected to propagate rapidly, introducing unforeseen problems elsewhere in the system. Sociologist Charles Perrow (1999) has developed a whole theory of accidents based on the idea that tight coupling can have catastrophic consequences, precisely as happened on this occasion. Use of the signal phone technology introduced a major perturbation into the system which ended up producing a catastrophic knock on effect. Designers of tightly coupled systems need to be acutely aware of the risks to safety and reliability that are inherent in such systems.

Examples of organisational risk-blindness

One very specific case of organisational risk-blindness contributed directly to the Glenbrook accident. Signallers generally had available to them an electronic "train indicator board", which automatically indicated the exact position of all trains in their area. There was, however, no such board in the signal box which covered the Glenbrook area. Signallers therefore had to rely on radio or phone communication to ascertain the position of trains in this area. This part of the track was described in evidence as a "dark area" or "no man's land". This very language suggests some level of awareness that the absence of a train indicator board constituted a risk. One could therefore say that this was not merely a case of risk-blindness but rather a more active matter of risk-denial on the part of the organisation. The fact is that if the signaller in the Glenbrook crash had had such a board available to him he would have known instantly that the *Indian Pacific* was in the way and would not have authorised the commuter train to proceed. The Commissioner highlighted this in his report: "The absence of a train indicator board ... was one of the major, if not the major cause, of this accident" (McInerney, 2000a:69).

It is worth mentioning certain other specific examples of organisational risk-blindness which came to light at the inquiry. A program was underway in 1997 to upgrade fire protection and warning systems for Sydney underground stations. Two stations had been upgraded when the funds ran out. A newly-arrived chief executive discovered that the two which had been upgraded were not the two which involved the greatest risk to the public. When he asked why, he was told that these two were the easiest to do. His comment to the inquiry was that this was "a very strange way in which to consider the allocation of capital funds", his point being that a risk-aware organisation would have dealt with the highest risk situations first.

This same executive provided a second example. He had spent new year's eve, one year, observing crowd management at Circular Quay station, a focal point for Sydney's new year activities:

> "What was interesting in the debriefing after that evening was that the line managers responsible for that area informed me that it had gone much better than it had done the previous year, and yet I had witnessed a number of occasions during the evening when platforms and concourse areas had become very dangerously overcrowded, where there was very high likelihood of injury to the passengers as a direct result."

It seems his line managers that night had been quite blind to the risks involved.

One of the other incidents investigated by the Glenbrook inquiry provided a glaring example of a lack of risk-awareness in engineering decision making. A number of signals in the metropolitan area are fitted with devices to derail a train that goes through a light at stop, in order to prevent the train moving into the path of another train. The incident in question was a derailment of this type, and the Commissioner observed that, had the train been travelling a little faster when it was derailed, "it could well have hit the overhead stanchion[3] and then plunged down an embankment with the obvious severe risk of death or injury to the driver and passengers on the train" (McInerney,

---

3   "Overhead stanchion" — the Commissioner is presumably referring to the structure which spans the tracks and carries the signal lights.

2001:98). No thought had been given during the installation of the system to the site where the train would "land" after derailment; the system design had not required any consideration of the possible consequences of the derailment. The Commissioner declared himself "mystified" by this extraordinary example of risk-blindness:

> "What I can't understand is why consideration wasn't given to that when the catch point was put in position. Surely that would be obvious to anybody, wouldn't it, if you are going to derail a train next to an overhead stanchion you might bring the whole thing down?"

Following the incident, an investigation was carried out of the 85 derailment points in the metropolitan area and 13 were found to be dangerous from this point of view and in need of modification (McInerney, 2001:98).

Risk and rules

A previous chapter demonstrated that the railway's reliance on rules to guide the behaviour of its front line staff had the effect of deadening risk-awareness. A mindful organisation must find a way to develop risk-awareness in its employees, but it must do so without abandoning rules. Strict compliance with some rules is vital. What must be abandoned is the presumption that rule making and even rule compliance are enough to guarantee safety. The Glenbrook inquiry turned into an extended investigation into how organisations can move away from an exclusive reliance on rules towards a more risk-focused approach, without at the same time abandoning all rules.

One important feature of the risk-focused approach is the hierarchy of controls, which stipulates that the first aim should be to eliminate risks from the work site, and only if this proves impossible should rules or procedures be relied on to protect people from the risks in question. A senior executive of the Queensland rail system explained that when he took up his job, track workers had been dying at the rate of two a year, but since introducing the hierarchy of controls, there had been no deaths for five years. Elimination of the risk in this context means that track workers are to be given exclusive possession of the track, in both directions, so that no trains run on the track while work is in progress. There are often time windows which make this possible and it is management's job to make best use of these. If that proves impossible, drivers will be notified of the need to slow down, and the site protected with small detonators placed on the track at some distance from the work site — trains explode the detonators when they run over them, reminding drivers of the need to slow down. In the context of the Glenbrook incident, the hierarchy of controls principle requires that efforts be made to eliminate the hazard of failed signals altogether rather than relying on rules which allow the signals at stop to be passed.

Even the most conscientious application of the hierarchy of controls can never eliminate the need for rules, and debate at the inquiry concerned what shape these rules should take. One witness spoke of the need for a small number of "golden rules" which must never be broken, such as a requirement that drivers always stop at red lights. Another suggested the following three "golden rules" for track workers:

- There shall always be a safe place for workers.

- Trains on adjacent tracks should not run at normal speed.

- For three or more adjacent tracks, special work-site protection must be provided.

A third witness spoke of the need for a small number of "fundamental principles", perhaps ten or less, from which procedures can be developed. He gave two examples: track workers and trains must always be separated, and electrical repair work must always be undertaken on disconnected circuitry.

But it is clear from these suggestions that the goal of a small number of rules will be elusive. The "golden rules" will need extensive elaboration and qualification if they are to be relatively unambiguous, and the "fundamental principles" will likewise give rise to a more extensive set of rules before they can be applied.

Another witness made a slightly different proposal. In any particular situation, the operator needs to have in his or her head a check list of actions to be taken. Rules need to be in dot point form and learnt by heart so that they appear in the mind as short commands in relevant situations. This is not the vision of a small number of golden rules but it shares with that formulation a concern for simplicity and immediate applicability.

None of these proposals, as articulated above, moves us significantly away from the existing strategy of identifying rules to cover every situation. The necessary additional ingredient is the idea that staff should carry out risk-assessments for themselves in each new situation they encounter. These risk-assessments might be guided by a small number of principles about the types of risks involved, but it would be up to the employees to apply these principles to the case at hand.

One senior executive said in relation to rail track workers, they should ask themselves four questions before they start work on the track:

- What's my job?

- Where am I doing it?

- What are the hazards associated with my job?

- Who is responsible for safety at this workplace?

He went on: "I have instructed ... my staff, if you don't get answers to these four questions, you don't start work."

Another executive described how the risk-management approach for rail track workers is now in two stages. The first is a planning phase in which the risks involved in carrying out the work are identified and controls are put in place to deal with these risks. For example, the job might be designed so that workers need never venture onto a live line or even into the space between the line under repair and the live line. Furthermore, hand signallers and detonators may be positioned to slow trains on live lines. The second phase occurs once workers reach the site. A briefing is given on how the job is to be done safely and any further risks identified and allowed for. It may turn out, for instance, that risks need to be re-evaluated in the light of unexpected weather.

Mention was made in Part A of "stop and think" and "take time, take charge" programs that various companies have implemented. All are designed to stimulate this kind of risk-awareness among their front line employees.

Imperfect though all these suggestions are, one can see in them an attempt to get away from a total reliance on rules towards strategies which promote risk-awareness among workers and their supervisors. According to the Queensland rail executive mentioned earlier, the greatest safety benefits arise from discussions, immediately prior to the job, about the risks that may be faced and the possible means of control.

For signallers and drivers, the risk-focused approach takes a slightly different form. Their jobs involve, for the most part, following fixed routines. The principles of risk management would require them to think consciously about risk every time there is any departure from normality. Thus, for example, if a train is to be diverted from its normal mainline route into a siding, the signaller responsible for setting the signal and points should consider the risks involved. An obvious risk is that the driver, not expecting to be diverted, will not see the signal and will enter the siding much too fast. A risk-aware signaller will contact the driver to warn of the route change.

Again, as a general principle, whenever the system is functioning in a degraded mode, that is, with some safety feature absent, all concerned should be asking the question: what are the risks involved in this form of operation? Passing a signal at stop is a case in point. Had the signaller in the Glenbrook crash asked himself about the risks of authorising the commuter train driver to proceed he would have been forced to consider the whereabouts of the *Indian Pacific*. As one inquiry witness put it, an alert should have been triggered when it became apparent that the status of the line ahead was unknown. Had the commuter train driver been similarly risk-aware he would have asked about the location of the *Indian Pacific*.

What, then, is the relationship between risk and rules? Does the strategy of encouraging risk-awareness do away with the need for rules? All witnesses were agreed that this was not the case. Most obviously, the practices of risk-awareness need themselves to be formulated as rules, for example, about when to be especially risk-aware.

The Commissioner at one point seemed to suggest, however, that neither rules nor risk management were really necessary; the problem was, he said, that "common sense is going out the window". He observed that there was a "growing industry" of risk management that "forgets the essential point":

> "... all sorts of words and phrases, ... definitions, people get bound up in that instead of using a bit of logic and common sense."

One can sympathise with the Commissioner's frustration. Safety management systems have sometimes been found to be theoretical edifices bearing little relation to what goes on in practice. Moreover, his views echo those of the report on the 1997 rail disaster at Southall in London which noted that risk-assessment was no "substitute for clear thinking" and no "substitute for common sense" (Uff, 2000:194,208).

However, common sense is not enough. Front line employees may be unaware of some risks or the most appropriate way to deal with them and, as one expert witness pointed out, what is required in these circumstances is a quite prescriptive check list of things to done. For instance, an electrician may not be aware of all the ways in which a piece of high-voltage equipment must be isolated before work on it can begin; in this case, there will be a need to follow a prescribed procedure precisely.

In some respects, what witnesses were proposing was that risk-awareness and rules be re-united. Rules, after all, had been developed to deal with the risks revealed by previous accidents. But employees were often unaware of the reason for the rules. If they studied the circumstances which had given rise to a rule they might be in a position to apply it in a more risk-aware way.

The absence of an informed culture

A central aspect of a risk-aware culture is that it is an informed culture (Reason, 1997:194). There are at least two major ways that organisations can inform themselves about risks. One is by good accident investigation and the other is by developing good risk-reporting systems. Both were effectively absent in the New South Wales rail system at the time of the Glenbrook accident.

In relation to accident investigation, we have already seen that the purpose of these investigations was to identify someone at fault. Once this had been done, the investigation was terminated. But human error or fault is the starting point for thorough investigation, not the end point. A good investigation will ask: why did the individual fail in the way he or she did; what were the error-enforcing conditions; and what were the organisational circumstances which contributed to the accident? To limit accident investigation to finding individual fault is not simply risk-blind, it amounts to the denial of risk (Cullen, 2001:73). The failure of the accident investigation system in this respect was demonstrated at the inquiry. Various examples of repeat accidents came to light, which indicated that there had been no effective learning from the first accident.

As for incident reporting, at the time of the Glenbrook accident a system called "trackwatch" was in existence. According to one expert witness, it simply didn't work. Drivers were asked to make oral reports to signallers. Signallers tended not to record these reports in written form but to ring some relevant person and pass on the report orally. Indeed, they actively resisted recording reports in writing. If drivers asked to have their reports formally recorded and assigned a number, they sometimes received such responses as: "We haven't been trained in that, mate." Or: "No, we don't bother about that. There is a ban on that." The lack of written recording meant that there was no systematic follow-up and no systematic compilation of the data. There was no possibility of learning from such a system.

Quite apart from the obstacles to reporting which signallers may have put in the way, drivers were discouraged from reporting by fear of reprisals. I have already mentioned a couple of extreme cases where disciplinary action was taken against drivers who made reports. More generally there was, among drivers, "a general perception that if you say nothing, you can't be 'had', and that you better be prepared to do battle if you speak up".

This was not a culture then in which effective steps where taken to become informed about risk. This was not an environment which encouraged organisational learning. This was yet another aspect of the blindness of the New South Wales rail system to risk.

Conclusion

The New South Wales rail system was risk-blind and frequently risk-denying. This chapter has sought to demonstrate this by sketching what a risk-aware rail system might look like, drawing on the expert opinion expressed at the inquiry. In so doing it has become clear that risk-awareness among front line workers is only one aspect of a risk-aware organisation. Individual risk-awareness depends on risk-awareness at the organisational level. A risk-blind organisation creates risk-blind individuals; in contrast, if the practices and procedures of an organisation focus on risk, its employees will come to do likewise. The discussion in this chapter is yet another demonstration, if one were needed, that culture is not just about mindset, it is about the practices of an organisation.

The abject failure of the rail system to respond to risk invites conclusions about a general organisational incompetence. When it came to the safety of track workers, in particular, the New South Wales railways had for years seemed almost paralysed and incapable of curtailing the toll of workers killed when hit by passing trains.

The chair of the Ladbroke inquiry, when confronted by a similar massive failure of risk-awareness, did indeed make use of terms that implied general organisational incompetence. Here are some of the phrases he used or endorsed: "a culture of apathy", "inadequate management", "an endemic culture of complacency", and an "unresponsive and slow moving" culture (Cullen, 2001:113,114,137).

It is tempting to apply these terms in the New South Wales' case, but this would be an unwarranted generalisation. While there was incompetence with respect to risk, one cannot talk of a general organisational incompetence. The railways were very effective when it came to on time running. Organisations which have the capacity to develop a culture of on time running also have the capacity to develop a culture of risk-awareness. It may be, however, that they will mobilise themselves in this way only when the external environment insists, as it has in the case of on time running.

Chapter 7
Glenbrook: concluding thoughts

One aspect of the New South Wales railway culture which so far has been implicit, must now be made explicit: it was a disempowering culture. It is important to recognise this because workforce empowerment is a precondition for risk-awareness.

Let us begin by considering why employee empowerment is such a necessity. Recall what it means to have a risk-aware workforce. A risk-aware worker is one who takes some degree of responsibility for his or her actions. The program at Western Mining, for example, was called "take time, take charge". Taking time may mean resisting pressures to get the job done as quickly as possible, and taking charge obviously requires that employees be empowered to make decisions about the way work is to be done.

An employee who takes charge may at times decide that the job should not be done because it cannot be done safely. Recall the rail executive who told track workers on his staff, "if you don't get answers to these four questions [about safety on the job], you don't start work". His workers are in a position to follow this instruction only if, when it comes to the point, they have been empowered to do so. This requires that immediate supervisors accept that it is legitimate for workers to decline to work in circumstances they view as dangerous, and this in turn means that senior managers must have conveyed to supervisors that they will support such decisions.

Risk-awareness among train drivers will take slightly different forms. It may mean making greater efforts to assemble relevant information from signallers about the whereabouts of trains, which in turn means questioning signallers more assertively. This will happen only if signallers have been trained about the need to maximise the information available to drivers, and drivers have been encouraged to take greater responsibility in this way. Or again, being risk-aware may mean declining to drive a train if it is discovered that safety relevant equipment is defective. Obviously, drivers will act in this way only if management from top to bottom accepts the legitimacy of such assertive behaviour.

Finally, it was stressed that a risk-aware organisation has an active incident-reporting system. This will work only if employees are encouraged to be on the look-out for things to report, and if their reports are responded to in a conscientious way. If employees are not empowered in this way, the organisation stands no chance of developing a culture of safety.

A culture of disempowerment

Given the importance of empowerment for safety, I want in this section to bring together some of the previous findings to suggest that the culture of the New South Wales railways was one which systematically disempowered employees.

The rule-focused nature of the culture discouraged workers from taking responsibility. Their job was to comply with the rules, as they understood them, and they were not encouraged to show initiative beyond this. So it was that the commuter train driver contented himself with seeking authorisation to pass the signal at stop and made no further inquiries. So it was, too, that when the driver of the *Indian Pacific* failed to get through to the signaller using the track-side phone at the second signal box, he accepted that failure and made no further effort to contact the signaller, even though he had in his train a modern communication system which would have enabled him to make contact. The rules forbade the use of this system and this prevented the driver displaying any further initiative. These two drivers were systematically disempowered by the railways' focus on rules.

The culture of blame contributed to the disempowerment of drivers in various ways. They ran the risk of being charged if they did anything without the proper authority. This obviously discouraged initiatives. They were also discouraged from reporting safety related matters: if you reported something, you might end up being blamed for it, so it was better to keep your head down and say nothing.

The organisational and occupational fragmentation of the workforce, referred to earlier as a "silo" phenomenon, further served to disempower employees. This was a culture which discouraged people from taking a broader view and from realising that their own behaviour impacted on others or that they might have a broader role in assuring the safety of others. The signallers were particularly disempowered in this respect, having a very blinkered view of their safety function. Similarly, each organisation was prevented by this culture from taking a system-wide view of its responsibilities.

The culture of on time running, for all its benefits, also disempowered employees, especially drivers, undermining their capacity to raise safety concerns, for example, about defective equipment. If such concerns interfered with on time running they were likely to be dismissed, sometimes in quite threatening ways.

Finally, the railways system was risk-blind, even risk-denying. Risk-denial directly undermined the capacity of employees to raise questions of safety.

The general effect of this disempowerment was to engender a sense of fatalism; that is, a feeling that accidents are inevitable and that there is nothing much that can be done about them. Leivesley (2000:2,11) notes that the rail culture was for the most part "reminiscent of the 19th century where accidents in the factories were accepted as inherent". She described it as "a culture of danger" which she defined as "an acceptance by persons of death and injury as inherent in their workplace"[1].

Other writers have used the concept of the culture of danger to explain the fatalism of miners, and such discussions normally assume that fatalism emerges as a way of enabling front line employees to cope with the dangers they encounter at the mine face (Fitzpatrick, 1974; Gouldner, 1954). Leivesley stresses, however, that the culture of danger, of fatalism, starts at the top, and changing it depends on changing the thinking of chief executives.

It is clear from this discussion that disempowerment of railway employees is a major impediment to improving safety. Until such time as employees are empowered to make safety-related decisions, any attempt to engender risk-awareness will be stillborn. To seek to create risk-awareness among employees who are systematically disempowered in their workplace is almost a contradiction in terms.

The paradox of empowerment in an authoritarian organisation

It was suggested during the inquiry that safety depended on developing even more authoritarian practices than existed in the railways. At first sight this might appear to be inconsistent with the need for greater empowerment. Surely an authoritarian organisation is one which disempowers its workforce? Let us consider this paradox.

Emergency services are organisations which must operate with a heightened awareness of risk, in order to maximise the safety of their own workers and also that of the public. An inquiry witness pointed out that these services function in a highly centralised way, with a high level of command and control by decision makers at the top of the organisational hierarchy. In some respects they function like military organisations, which are of course classic authoritarian organisations. A crucial part of emergency service organisations, the witness said, is an effective communication network which serves to "bind people together ... and ensure that the operations are under a single line of command so that no-one decides to vary things on their own cognisance". It does not follow from this, however, that front line workers are disempowered. In fact, they are specifically empowered to take initiatives and vary procedures in certain circumstances, but they must communicate to command headquarters what it is they are doing. Moreover, emergency service employees are intensively trained in how to perform their functions and how to exercise initiative when it is called for. In short, highly centralised, authoritarian organisations *can* leave scope for employee initiatives which naturally encourage risk-awareness.

---

1 Statement to the inquiry, pp 2,11.

Various witnesses argued that the railways need to exercise greater effective control over employees by training them more intensively and testing them in the field under varying conditions, especially degraded or unusual conditions. Moreover, rules need to be quite prescriptive, not of every action to be taken in every situation, but of the kinds of decisions which must be taken and the information to be considered. This was clearly not an argument for the further disempowerment of front line workers.

Confirmation that even the most authoritarian organisations can nevertheless empower their workforces comes from research on decision making on board American nuclear aircraft carriers (LaPorte and Consolini, 1991). Decision making in this context is normally highly centralised, but in times of crisis, or very high tempo, such as when large numbers of aircraft are landing on the deck in quick succession, decision making migrates to people lower down the hierarchy, who are best equipped to make those decisions. Of course, decisions are made in accordance with clearly understood guidelines and people are drilled in these until they are second nature, but these very guidelines empower people at the front line to make crucial decisions. In short, despite the authoritarian, hierarchical nature of the organisation, the decision-making process is quite flexible and varies with the circumstances.

As noted in Part A, several writers have argued that flexible decision making is one of the hallmarks of a culture of safety or of mindful organisations. Such flexibility involves the empowerment of front line workers and the examples provided here suggest that this is possible even in the most hierarchical of organisations.

The causes of the crash

It was noted in Chapter 2 that this discussion has been organised around four cultural themes. An alternative mode of organisation would have been to focus on the causes of the accident and to analyse them in a systematic fashion. A causal analysis is of course implied in the previous discussion and it is made more explicit in the following diagram (see Fig 1). The diagram displays the main causes touched on above[2] and shows how they interrelate. It is constructed by starting with the crash and asking "why?". The questioning is continued until the cultural causes are reached. Further questioning reveals some of the sources of these cultural phenomena. Each factor along the way is arguably a necessary condition, in the sense that, had this factor been otherwise the accident probably would not have occurred (Hopkins, 2000a: Ch 9). The diagram is divided into three layers: specific causes, cultural causes and sources of culture. There is nothing pre-ordained about these categories — they arise naturally from the particular analysis conducted here.[3]

---

2   Not all the causes discussed in the inquiry are displayed in this diagram.

3   This style of analysis is inspired by Rasmussen's "accimaps" (Rasmussen, 1997).

Figure 1: Causes of the Glenbrook train crash

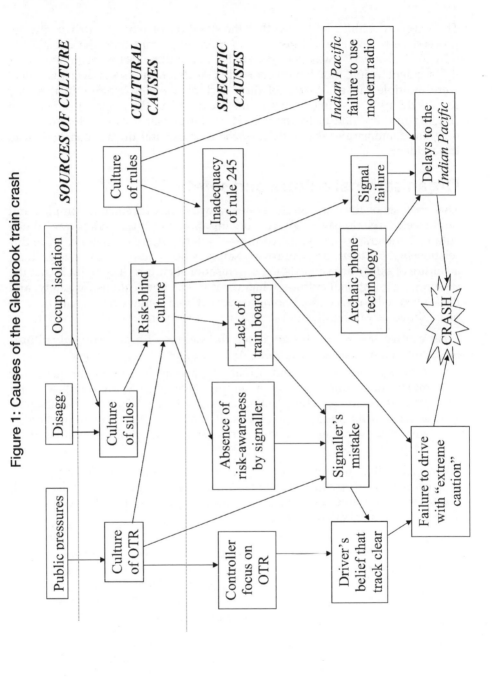

The diagram enables us to see that the question of why the driver did not proceed with "extreme caution" is no more important than the question of why the *Indian Pacific* was delayed. Had either of these factors been otherwise, the accident would not have occurred. The diagram also shows that there were multiple causes of each of these factors. Viewing matters in this way reveals the truly systemic nature of the accident and the inappropriateness of singling out any one factor or person as the primary cause. Moreover, the diagram demonstrates explicitly how the four cultural themes contributed to the accident.

Organisational culture and safety

This analysis of the New South Wales railways has revealed a complex and multifaceted relationship between organisational culture and safety. While culture is integral to safety, the concept of safety culture does not capture this relationship. Furthermore, improving safety is not simply a matter of grafting a culture of safety onto an existing organisational culture. The point is that the existing organisational culture, whatever it is, has implications for safety, and these need to be understood. Some aspects of an existing culture may need to be modified before significant safety improvements are possible.

What can we say, in conclusion, about the sources of organisational culture? First, cultures are created by leaders. As the Glenbrook report notes:

> "Management actions and actual day to day behaviour are generally much more important than simply changing written policies and procedures for effecting lasting cultural change. For senior managers, actions speak louder than words. If senior management only changes what it says, rather than what it does, then little progress will be made (McInerney, 2001:49)."

Second, the ultimate source of organisational culture may lie outside the organisation. It is public pressure which has focused the minds of rail executives on on time running; similar external pressure may be necessary to generate equivalent attention to risk.

part C

Organisational Culture and Safety
in the Royal Australian Air Force

Chapter 8

Introduction to the Royal Australian Air Force case study

The problem

From the late 1970s, Royal Australian Air Force (RAAF) maintenance personnel worked inside the fuel tanks of F111 fighter bombers in an ongoing series of repair programs. They worked in cramped and very unpleasant conditions, sometimes in unbearable heat and sometimes in near freezing temperatures, and they suffered prolonged and sometimes intense exposure to the toxic chemicals with which they worked. By 2000, the health of more than 400 people had been ruined and the Air Force finally realised it had a serious problem on its hands.

Workers suffered from a wide variety of ailments that in retrospect were clearly attributable to chemical exposure, although they did not always make the connection at the time. Among these were skin irritation, gastrointestinal problems, loss of interest in sex, rapid mood swings, headaches, dizziness, haemorrhoids, skin cancers, and loss of memory. Various memory loss stories circulated: one, for example, was about a man who had experienced difficulty getting the soap to lather in the shower, and eventually realised that he had not turned the water on. While workers recognised the funny side of such stories, they were also alarmed at what was happening to them. Many of these people have had to retire prematurely and now lead miserable lives.

A high powered Board of Inquiry was convened to examine just why it was that the Air Force had failed for such an extended period of time to safeguard the health of its members. I was a member of this Board.[1] Our inquiry brought to light a number of aspects of Air Force culture which had systematically undermined safety throughout this whole period. This was despite various initiatives which the Air Force had taken to improve the management of safety. The case is therefore a powerful illustration of one the central claims of this book; namely, that attempts to enhance safety can be entirely negated by existing features of an organisation's culture, and that these features need to be tackled directly before real safety improvement can be achieved. Part C of

---

1   The Air Force is to be congratulated for appointing an external person to the Board. In so doing it demonstrated that it wished to get to the bottom of what had happened, no matter how uncomfortable that might be. The Board's report (Report of the F111 Deseal/Reseal Inquiry) was indeed disquieting, but its recommendations were accepted and structures have been put in place to implement them.

this book is a re-working of the Board of Inquiry report (Clarkson, Hopkins and Taylor, 2001)[2] to highlight the impact of the organisational culture of the Air Force on safety.

The protection failures

Soon after the Air Force took delivery of its F111s in the early 1970s, it became apparent that the chemicals used to seal the inside of the fuel tanks deteriorated rapidly, allowing fuel to leak out. Maintenance workers therefore had to crawl inside the tanks and apply various toxic desealants and then resealants, often by hand, and sometimes by spray. They were supposed to be protected from these chemicals by gloves, respirators and impermeable suits, but this equipment proved to be ineffective. The difficulties that workers experienced with this personal protective equipment (PPE) are worth reviewing in some detail.

The gloves sometimes disintegrated within five minutes of contact with the chemicals, and rather than constantly stopping to put on new gloves, workers at times chose to continue work without them. Moreover, some of the work required considerable manual dexterity. The gloves reduced dexterity and so workers sometimes had to remove them or cut the fingers off the gloves to get the job done.

Respirators were supposed to protect workers from toxic fumes. The respirators came with renewable filters. Sometimes the only filters available were dust particle filters, which were ineffective against chemical fumes. Workers had no option but to put up with these filters and suffered headaches and other symptoms at these times. Moreover, at times, when workers were in very confined spaces, the respirators impeded their ability to perform their tasks and they felt they had no option but to remove them to carry out the work.

The protective suits they were given were also inadequate in many ways. During the last of the programs, which involved spray sealing, and for which protective suits were particularly important, it turned out the material of which the suits were made was semi-permeable to two of the chemicals in use.

Not only was the equipment defective in these ways, it was also highly uncomfortable. The work was carried out at Amberley Air Force base near Brisbane, and temperatures in the maintenance hangar and inside the fuel tanks were often very high during summer. One worker described wearing a protective suit inside a fuel tank as like being "dressed up in a couple of

---

2   The other two members of the Board of Inquiry bear no responsibility for this re-working. The re-working will quote liberally from the Board's report, but to avoid cluttering the text, some of these quotations will not be specifically acknowledged. The Chief of the Air Force has provided copyright release for the use the report in this way.

overcoats in the middle of summer crawling around in your kitchen cupboards". In these circumstances, workers sometimes chose not to wear the equipment provided for them.

But it was not just the PPE which was problematic. There was supposed to be a ventilation system in the hangars in which the work was occurring, but this was switched off at 4 pm on weekdays and was not available at all during weekends. Nevertheless, overtime was often required during these periods, so work was done without ventilation, resulting in a far greater risk of exposure to chemicals.

As a result of these numerous deficiencies in the protective systems, workers suffered chronic and sometimes acute exposure. There were various occasions on which workers were overcome by fumes in the tanks and had to be pulled out, unconscious. Moreover, in the early days of the program, desealing was done with a particularly foul smelling chemical, SR51, and after using this chemical, workers' bodies would stink for days, despite all attempts to wash it off. These workers were banned from the mess because of their offensive odour. Here was clear evidence that protective measures were not effective and that workers were absorbing the toxic substance in question into their bodies, yet no one in authority appeared to understand this, or to be perturbed.

The lack of response

The Air Force as a whole failed to respond to these problems until early in 2000, when so many workers were seeking medical attention that Air Force doctors began to take an interest in what was happening in the workplace. Until that time, Air Force doctors had treated people with medications and sent them away. Even on occasions when workers sought medical assistance after passing out in the fuel tanks, doctors did no more than medicate them.

Most of the occupational health and safety (OHS) audits which were done in the fuel tank repair section failed to identify the problems which workers were experiencing with the PPE, and those that did failed to trigger any serious response. None of the health problems and none of the problems with the PPE was reported through any of the Air Force's incident and hazard reporting systems.

Senior officers were unaware of the problems being experienced in the fuel tank repair section and simply assumed that they would have been alerted to anything of significance. Their comments to the Board of Inquiry revealed that they placed a great deal of faith in their system. They are worth repeating in some detail. According to one:

"I expected that, having provided a command and management framework, appropriate direction, priorities and resources to my subordinate commanders and supervisors, they are then responsible and accountable for discharging their duties. Such accountability also requires that should difficulties be experienced in carrying out tasks, either personally assigned by me as the officer commanding or injected laterally into the organisation from outside agencies, such difficulties are to be brought to my attention ...

I feel confident that should a serious safety concern be identified, it would have been raised through the management chain rapidly (Clarkson, Hopkins and Taylor, 2001:3-1)."

And here are the words of a second:

"I believe that the ingrained requirement to follow procedures and to supervise subordinates to ensure that this is done is such as to make instances of non-compliance the exception.

I have no reason to believe that the procedures developed for the Deseal/Reseal were not generally followed. I consider that the supervisory chain and the Air Force emphasis on supervision was sufficient to ensure compliance with procedures ... (Clarkson, Hopkins and Taylor, 2001:3-2)."

However, despite such convictions, it is clear that the chain of command did not function to alert senior commanders to the problems in the fuel tank repair section, and that the supervisory processes failed to secure compliance with the requirements that adequate PPE be provided and worn at all times.

The record, then, is one of dismal failure with respect to the health of the workers in the F111 fuel tank repair section. The question which cries out for an answer is how this situation could have been allowed to persist for so long. The Air Force is not a heartless organisation. Fuel tank workers were Air Force "members" and the Air Force had a policy of looking after its own.[3] How could its health and safety management system have failed so totally? To answer this question requires a fairly detailed examination of the culture of the Air Force, to which I now turn.

---

3   There is an important difference between the RAAF and the USAF in this respect. The USAF F111s experienced the same fuel leak problems, but much of the fuel tank repair work was done by itinerant workers, many of whom were illegal immigrants. Not surprisingly, no information has been found about any health problems they might have.

Chapter 9

Aspects of Air Force culture

There are several fundamental values which contributed to the incapacity of the Air Force to recognise and respond to what was happening to its fuel tank workers. This chapter deals with some of these values and shows how they contributed to the problem. The Royal Australian Air Force (RAAF) is a large organisation, with many of the strengths and weaknesses of other large organisations, particularly large industrial organisations, and some values identified here will be found in other, non-military organisations. An examination of these values is therefore of relevance beyond the military. The values discussed are: the priority of operations over logistics, the "can do" attitude, the priority of platforms over people, and the command and discipline system.

The priority of operations over logistics

The distinction between operations and logistics is one of the fundamental cleavage lines of the Air Force. *Operations* refers to all flying activities of the aircraft squadrons, including training. *Logistics* refers to activities which support operations and includes aircraft maintenance work. Some maintenance work is done by personnel attached to the flying squadrons, but the more extensive maintenance, including much of the fuel tank repair work, has been done by maintenance organisations with no operational role. The distinction between operations and logistics is therefore not only a conceptual one; it is mirrored in the way the Air Force is organised.

In almost every way, operations takes precedence over logistics. The needs of the operational squadrons drive the activities of the logistics squadrons. Operations is what the Air Force is about, and the *raison d'etre* of logistics is to serve operations. The motto on the letterhead of the maintenance wing at Amberley was "excellent logistics for operations".

Pilots are trained to think of themselves as the elite of the Air Force and it is significant that Air Force chiefs have always been drawn from the ranks of pilots. Maintenance workers are drawn into this value system and reproduce it in subtle ways. For instance, they feel a sense of pride when an aircraft they have worked on takes to the skies. The whole status system within the Air Force, then, emphasises the priority of operations.

Production pressures

The aim of a maintenance squadron or wing is to produce serviceable aircraft for use by operating squadrons. In this respect, a maintenance organisation within the Air Force is driven by production imperatives in the same way as any private sector producer. It must meet the needs of its client operating squadrons in the same way that private sector producers must supply the needs of their customers. A suspension of the maintenance program at Amberley would mean a failure in the supply of serviceable aircraft to the client, just as the disruption of electricity or gas production results in a failure of supply to customers. Such a failure would disrupt the training programs being conducted by operating groups and this leads to enormous pressures on maintenance groups to do whatever it takes to get aircraft back into the air. This is the real source of the pressure on maintenance workers and their immediate supervisors to put up with defective equipment and conditions in order to get on with the job, for to do otherwise might compromise fundamental Air Force goals. Put another way, it is the source of the "can do" attitude that pervades maintenance sections, to be discussed in more detail shortly.

The failure of the medical services

The priority of operations over logistics also contributed, very directly, to the failure of Air Force doctors to recognise and respond to the problems experienced in the fuel tank repair section. A senior Air Force doctor described the situation as follows:

> "The operational demands of RAAF Amberley were extremely high. ... There were enormous pressures to focus output on the operational squadrons ... The main priority of the Base Medical Flight was personnel with aircrew status. This meant the re-validation of aircrew medicals. Aircrew consisted of pilots, navigators and flight engineers, air traffic controllers and air defence operators. Aircrew ... were given priority for medical treatment if ill or injured.

> The second highest priority was the treatment of injuries and disease. ... The focus of this activity was to minimise illness and to rehabilitate members after injury to maximise their fitness for duty.

> The third level of priority were medical assessments and monitoring of non-aircrews (Clarkson, Hopkins and Taylor, 2001:2-3)."

The Air Force also had a so-called "environmental health program". Its priorities were specified in writing, with top priority given to the health of pilots, a lower priority to public health issues such as water supply, food hygiene and disease and insect control, and the lowest priority to the health issues of maintenance and other support workers.

So it was that, when these workers visited the medical centre complaining of symptoms which, at least in retrospect, were clearly related to their occupational environment, they were treated for the symptoms with no recognition that these might be occupationally induced.

The dearth of engineering officers

The priority of operations over logistics manifested itself further in the proportions of officers in each area. Officers in the maintenance organisations were qualified engineers; officers in the operational organisations were trained pilots. Junior officers in maintenance sections had large numbers of people under their control, including non-commissioned officers, corporals and so-called "aircraftmen", who were not in fact flyers but tradesmen and women of various kinds. On the other hand, junior flying officers had almost no one under their command. Moreover, cost cutting in recent years had fallen disproportionately on the engineering officers whose numbers had been so reduced that they were incapable of exercising effective control over the maintenance activities for which they were responsible. For instance, at one relevant period the junior engineering officer in charge of the fuel tank repair section was responsible for six other maintenance groups as well. He had a total of 170 personnel under his authority, even though he had not had any significant management experience. Because of this breadth of responsibility, he had very little idea of what was happening in the fuel tank repair section, which in reality was left to manage itself. More precisely, it was left to the flight sergeants and other non-commissioned officers in the section to manage as best they could with the resources available to them.

It is not surprising, therefore, that this young officer did not know that unauthorised work practices had developed in the section, nor did he know of the difficulties workers had had with the personal protective equipment (PPE). Moreover, he had no knowledge of the symptoms of exposure to toxic chemicals from which the workers under his command suffered throughout this period.

In short, the priority of operations over logistics meant that the maintenance section was systematically deprived of expert engineering input or supervision. It was a priority which undermined the Air Force's capacity to manage effectively what was happening on the hangar floor.

The dangers of running down engineering expertise have been noted in other contexts. The Royal Commission into the gas plant explosion at Longford, Victoria found that the withdrawal of engineers from site as a cost-cutting measure had led to inadequate supervision of trade staff, which in turn contributed to the accident (Dawson and Brooks, 1999). Engineers are a resource which must be available in technically complex environments to provide back-up to those who are more directly involved in the production process. Unfortunately, there is quite a widespread failure to recognise this vital engineering role. The result is that, when things appear to be running smoothly, there is a tendency to cut engineering staff on the grounds that they are to some extent redundant. Time and again, however, this has been shown to be a false economy (Yates, 2000).

The "can do" attitude

The phenomenon of making do with available resources and, if necessary, deviating from required safety procedures in order to get the job done, so very much in evidence in the fuel tank repair section, is sometimes described as a "can do" philosophy. This is a second major value orientation which contributed to the fate of the fuel tank workers.

The Air Force was very well aware of this orientation and the impact it was having. One senior Air Force commander expressed the problem in the following terms:

> "For some time, there has been general agreement across the RAAF that it is under-resourced (in funding and personnel) and over-tasked. ... The result has been the strong inculcation of a "can do" mentality within management [at all levels] which largely requires people to do the best they can and to advise management when they cannot meet the task.
>
> Recent surveys indicate that the "can do" mentality is so strong (now perhaps "must do"), that even at the levels where maintenance work is actually being conducted people are extraordinarily reluctant to admit that tasks cannot be achieved. Evidence suggests that short cuts may be being used to achieve tasks in the belief that this is accord with the overall aim of the unit/RAAF (to achieve output — aircraft on line — in the minimum time). ...
>
> There is a serious and challenging dichotomy between the views of the practitioners of aircraft maintenance and RAAF management. In effect, the troops feel they are doing the right thing, whilst management do not condone at all the range of expedient practices being employed (Clarkson, Hopkins and Taylor, 2001:4-5)."

The immediate supervisors of fuel tank repair workers played a critical role in propagating the "can do" attitude. They did so through no fault of their own; they found themselves in an untenable position of being required to get the job done in a situation over which they had little control. As one commented:

> "I am aware of occasions when troop members removed the respirators from their face because they could not wear them in confined areas in some of the fuselage tanks. Working conditions inside the tanks were always difficult, but the job had to be done ..."

And according to another:

> "The troops knew the gloves did not work, but the troops had to keep going to get the job done ..."

One of these supervisors experimented with 15 different types of glove in a desperate effort to find a way to protect his workers. Work continued throughout this period of experimentation, as it had to, and in the end, none of the gloves was found to be effective. One can readily sympathise with the dilemma in which this supervisor found himself.

In short, although the Air Force was aware of the "can do" problem and of the fact that people would tolerate dangerous conditions or bend the rules in various ways to get the job done, it had not been able to translate this awareness into effective action to protect the health of the fuel tank repair workers.

Many organisations value a "can do" attitude and seek to inculcate it in their employees. In particular, when organisations downsize, employees are effectively asked to do more with less, and will often do the best they can, even if it means exposing themselves and others to risks which the organisation at a policy level views as unacceptable. The Air Force experience demonstrates just how badly things can go wrong if "can do" is not tempered by other considerations.

"Can do" is not an entirely negative phenomenon. It is an attitude which encourages initiative and self-reliance which, in many contexts, are highly desirable traits. The challenge is to ensure that initiative and self-reliance do not degenerate into corner cutting and undue risk taking.

The issue of micro-management

The "can do" attitude is closely related to two other attitudes which were in evidence at Amberley. The first is that it is not appropriate for senior management to micro-manage, and the second, in some sense a corollary of the first, is that people should seek to solve problems at their own level without involving more senior management.

The idea that senior managers should not "micro-manage" those below them is prominent in management theory. Subordinates have a job to do and should be left alone as far as possible to get on with it. To do otherwise is to undermine them. So, for example, when a United States submarine surfaced under a Japanese fishing vessel, killing nine people, due in part to a failure of a crew member to carry out his usual function, the Commander defended himself by saying:

> "I depended on my subordinates to ensure that watches were properly staffed and that provisions were made for working around broken equipment. I didn't micro-manage my crew. I empowered them to do their job (Clarkson, Hopkins and Taylor, 2001:3-4)."

A similar presumption against micro-management operated at Amberley. After making reference to this concept at the inquiry, a wing commander explained:

> "I would try and look at a higher level of dealing with things than the squadron leader's. And it is not my job to do the squadron leader's job."

The other side of this particular coin is that people are not expected to take matters to their superiors unless they feel unable handle them. As the junior engineering officer quoted above noted:

> "The system was such that only those problems which could not be rectified at that level [below me] should be brought to my attention."

For a subordinate to bring an issue to the attention of a superior was in some respects an admission of failure, which naturally encouraged the subordinate to get the job done with the resources at hand.

There is of course a competing view about the most effective way to manage. Senior managers need to know what is going on at lower levels in their organisations and, as the Secretary of Defence himself observed:

> "It is notoriously difficult for the heads of large organisations to get direct, unsanitised feedback from people who do not report directly to them (Hawke, 2000)."

Managers need to find ways to assure themselves that information about things which are going wrong, or procedures which are not being followed, is indeed able to find its way up the management chain. One simple strategy, which management theorists all agree is critical, is that senior managers should regularly take the time to walk around workplaces and talk to people in informal ways, so as to give them the opportunity to voice concerns or grievances. This was certainly an aspect of management strategy at Amberley, in theory. In practice, however, it seemed to have had a relatively low priority, for according to the evidence of workers on the shop floor, they very rarely saw a senior officer and even more rarely had any opportunity to talk with one. Moreover, visits by senior officers tended not to be "walk-arounds" for the purpose of observation and casual interaction, but occasions for addressing the troops and providing them with information. These are very different activities.

It seems that the balance struck by management at Amberley between the need to avoid micro-managing and the need to make direct contact with lower ranks was far from optimal.

In summary, without recognising what they were doing, senior managers actively encouraged a "can do" attitude among maintenance workers by their systematic lack of attention to what was going on on the hangar floor. This is a clear illustration of the point made in the Introduction to this book, that leaders create cultures by their own behaviour.

The priority of platforms over people

At about the time the Board of Inquiry was sitting, the Secretary of the Department of Defence gave an address entitled "People Power", in which he raised the issue of people versus platforms (weapons platforms, eg aircraft or ships). Defence, he said, was sometimes criticised as being too "platform-centric" (Hawke, 2000) and he argued that there was a need to put people first. He took issue with those who say that equipment must remain the primary focus, and argued that without a "people first" culture, recruitment and retention rates would decline and with them the ability to sustain operational capability. "People matter — it's people who make the difference", he said. In so saying, the Secretary of Defence was seeking to reverse traditional priorities. Those priorities had no doubt been driven by the relative costs of replacing platforms and people, but they were now, he was suggesting, counter-productive.

The traditional priority of platforms ahead of people was in evidence at Amberley. It can be very simply and poignantly illustrated by the case of one worker who was employed to dispose of a chemical used in the first repair program in the 1970s. SR51 was a toxic substance used to strip away the old and disintegrating sealants inside the tanks, prior to resealing. After use it was disposed of by means of incineration, in a remote corner of the base. This was a lonely and unsupervised activity and the worker whose job this was throughout 1979-1980 spent much of his time covered in this chemical. Throughout this period he suffered various ill-effects including memory loss, mood swings and vertigo. He complained from time to time about these symptoms but nothing was done about his conditions of work. On one matter, however, the Air Force was particular. He was not to operate the incinerator at any time an F111 was taking off, so as to avoid any possibility that the combustion products from the incinerator might damage the aircraft. There is no suggestion here that a deliberate decision was made to give greater importance to an aircraft than to an individual; it is simply that the well-being of the aircraft was attended to while the well-being of the individual was not.

This priority contributed in a number of important ways to the situation in which the fuel tank workers found themselves. The Air Force went to great lengths to ensure that the deseal/reseal process which it had designed was as effective as possible in reducing fuel leaks; it did not go to corresponding lengths to ensure the effectiveness of the protection which was provided for fuel tank workers. In the first program, for instance, the Air Force turned to an expert in sealant chemistry for advice on resealing the fuel tanks. However, it then expected him to double as a toxicologist, which he was not, and to certify the safety of the chemicals he was proposing. It is inconceivable that it would have employed a toxicologist for safety advice and then asked him to double as a sealant chemist. Furthermore, this expert was asked to visit and give advice when sealants did not cure properly, or when there were other quality control issues, but no similar visits from external authorities were sought in relation to problems being experienced with PPE.

The quality control in relation to the sealant application was extensive, and effective. According to the outside expert:

"The remarkably low incidence of leaks to date contrasts most favourably with the USAF experience and is a tribute to the care and attention to quality control that has been adopted at Amberley."

But there was no equivalent quality control in relation to the use of protective equipment. As the Board put it:

"Until the Air Force puts the same effort into securing expert safety advice as it does into securing expert advice on materials, until it applies the same level of quality control to ensuring the safety of maintenance workers as it applies to ensuring the adequacy of maintenance processes, it will remain vulnerable to the criticism that it puts platforms ahead of people (Clarkson, Hopkins and Taylor, 2001:6-3)."

There is another way of talking about the impact of this platform-centric attitude. It is far better to eliminate hazards when equipment or processes are designed, than to rely on personal equipment to protect workers from these hazards. There is in fact a hierarchy of controls for dealing with hazards, ranging from elimination, at the top, through engineering and administrative controls, to the use of PPE at the bottom. The deseal/reseal programs relied very heavily on PPE to safeguard workers. The programs were designed with the needs of the aircraft in mind, the assumption being that any hazards generated in the process could be compensated for by the use of PPE. One consequence of this approach was that no serious attempt was made to identify and use non-toxic chemicals. There was evidence, for instance, that in some circumstances detergent and hot water was just as effective for removing old sealant as was the toxic solvent that was actually used, but it seems no consideration was ever given to this alternative. In short, although the Air Force recognised the hierarchy of controls in various of its publications, no attempt was made to apply this hierarchy in the deseal/reseal programs. The absence of any commitment to the hierarchy of controls is another manifestation of the priory of platforms over people.

Shortly after our inquiry, a striking example came to light of the way the priority of platforms over people had operated in the Australian Navy during the Vietnam War (NRCET, 2002). I tell this story because it underlines just how pervasive this value appears to be. The Navy's ships needed to draw water from overboard, both for drinking and for use in the ships' boilers. This water had to be distilled before use, to remove salt. Navy patrols spent considerable amounts of time in estuarine waters in Vietnam which were known to be contaminated with other substances and there was a possibility that distillation would not remove these contaminants. The Navy therefore chose not to use distilled water from the estuaries for its boilers, lest it damage ships' engines; water for the boilers was to be produced only from the pristine waters offshore. Distilled water from the estuaries could, however, be used as drinking water!

In fact, the estuaries were contaminated with agent orange, which was used as a defoliant in the war, and some of the constituents of agent orange were carcinogenic. Ironically, the distillation process served only to concentrate these substances, and this is what the sailors were drinking. Studies have shown that the death rates among naval veterans from this period are significantly higher than normal, higher even than for other veteran groups, and contaminated drinking water appears to be the most likely explanation. The Navy had attended to the welfare of its platforms in this matter, but not its people, with tragic consequences.

Command and discipline

Many of the aspects of Air Force culture so far identified as contributing to the exposure of troops to hazardous chemicals are present in other large organisations. However, there is one feature of military culture not present in civilian organisations — the command and discipline system. The command and discipline system exists for very good reason — one can hardly imagine a military campaign being fought on any other basis — and the military is imbued with the importance of a strict obedience to higher authority.

There is no doubt that fuel tank workers worked under the threat of disciplinary action. As one said:

> "I recall one of the fellows got his brother who worked in a lab in Melbourne to test it (SR51) and he was told to get out of the Section as quickly as possible. We accepted that opinion rather than the medical opinion, but there was little we could do about it because we were under strict orders. If we asked to be transferred we were told that we had to do our time, which was two years at that stage (Clarkson, Hopkins and Taylor, 2001:9-1)."

Another witness gave the following evidence:

> "As a junior tradesman I just did what I was told by my NCO and supervisors. I was constantly assured that everything I did with the chemicals was safe and there was no cause for concern. It is my belief that the consequence of not undertaking the tasks that I was given completely would be that I would be subject to contact counselling (that is, I would be taken out the back and given a clip under the ear). It was just as though it was a requirement for any new member of the unit whenever posted in to do their time in the Deseal/Reseal section. It was a culture within the unit that you could not bring up and raise any concerns and you simply did what you were told or got a kick in the arse (Clarkson, Hopkins and Taylor, 2001:9-1)."

These perceptions were not unfounded. In the first deseal/reseal program, one worker who refused to re-enter the fuel tanks was charged with an offence, convicted and sentenced to seven days detention at Amberley.

An Air Force review of the maintenance work at Amberley in 1979 expressed some concern about this situation:

> "In winter this is cold, cheerless, obnoxious and very demanding work ... Several psychological problems have already emerged among airmen engaged in this extremely unpopular, but necessary work. There should be no need to reiterate the importance that the nation places on this work and neither is there any reason to doubt the motivation of those employed on it. But when considering the conditions under which they work, for peacetime, it could be argued that their loyalty is being unreasonably tested (Clarkson, Hopkins and Taylor, 2001:9-1)."

The Board had no evidence of disciplinary action being taken in more recent years to compel people to work in the fuel tank repair section, but the threat was always there if they refused.

While the principles of command and discipline in an operational setting are essential, these same principles in a peacetime industrial setting, such as a large maintenance base, seem far more questionable, especially in view of the unfortunate consequences they can have. At Amberley they contributed to the suppression of the health problems which fuel tank repair workers experienced.

The importance the military and the government places on command and discipline has led to the weakening of the legislative protection afforded to Service personnel. The Services operate under the umbrella of the *Occupational Health and Safety (Commonwealth Employment) Act 1991* (OHS Act), but this Act provides for the exemption of Defence from various of its provisions. In particular, the employee empowerment provisions of the Act do not apply to the Services, on the ground that they empower employees to challenge their superiors in ways which would be inconsistent with the military command system. In civilian contexts, occupational health and safety representatives are elected by groups of workers and they are provided with powers under the Act, among them the power to issue provisional improvement notices. These notices can require employers to take action to deal with contraventions or hazardous situations. If the employer disputes a notice, it may call in a government inspector to adjudicate. The aim of this provision is to empower workers to take action, against employer resistance, in relation to health and safety matters, and it is prima facie inconsistent with the military command system.

The Australian Defence Force (ADF) recognised that, on the face of it, the removal of the apparatus of worker empowerment appeared to deprive employees of one of their protections. But its position was that:

> "The basic intent of those aspects of the OHS Act is achievable in the ADF in ways that are more compatible with the military command and discipline system and which reflect both the authority, and the responsibility for the health and welfare of subordinates implicit in the function of command."

The Air Force sought to implement this policy by defining each work group as a "safety improvement team", with the non-commissioned officer in charge of the group defined as a safety improvement team leader. This team leader was seen as the rough equivalent of the health and safety representative envisaged in the Act.

There is an important difference, however. The team leader was a part of the normal chain of command, rather than standing in some sense outside of it, as do civilian health and safety representatives. So, if the chain of command is failing to attend appropriately to health and safety, safety improvement team leaders do not offer any additional protection for workers because they are part of that fallible chain.

Interestingly, a Defence report on equity issues made a similar point. It concluded that the system of equity officers did not work because the equity officers were part of the chain of command and it recommended "that officers in the direct chain of command and senior non-commissioned officers responsible for the discipline system in units not be appointed as Equity Officers. The two roles cannot be adequately reconciled" (JSTFADT, 2001:59).

A further problem with safety improvement team leaders was that they were at sergeant level or above, and hence, somewhat removed from the hangar floor. This meant that they were not in a position to see things in the way that corporals and leading aircraftmen and women might, and would not necessarily enjoy the confidence of junior ranks in the way that an elected health and safety representative might be expected to. Nor were they exposed to the hazards of the work process to the extent that the more junior ranks were. This detracted from their ability to raise issues from the hangar floor.

The command and control system is restricted to the Defence Forces and one or two other organisations such as the police. But there are obviously parallels in civilian employment generally. Employees often feel that, if they wish to keep their jobs, they have no choice but to comply with requirements which may be undermining their health. The threat of losing one's job may be every bit as powerful as the threat of military discipline. Perhaps the difference is that the compulsion which civilian employees experience is not legitimated by a value system in the way that it is in the Defence Forces.

Conclusion

This chapter has identified a number of Air Force values which operated to undermine its stated commitment to OHS. These values are not wholly undesirable. The priority of operations, the value placed on getting the job done ("can do"), and the importance of command and control, all serve the basic purposes of the organisation. The challenge is to find ways to temper these values to ensure that they do not have the detrimental effects they did at Amberley. One value does appear to be wholly undesirable, that of the priority of platforms over people.

The Air Force has accepted much of the Board's analysis. The Chief of the Air Force announced in a policy statement following the report that:

> "... the Air Force has a duty of care and a moral obligation to manage and protect the safety of our most valuable asset — our people. This stems from legislation ... and from Air Force values."

In so saying, he was clearly attempting to repudiate the traditional priority of platforms over people. He went on:

> "... in our current peacetime environment, the loss of any of our people or an aircraft is not acceptable. In higher risk military operations, we must control the risks and ensure we maintain our cultural perception of 'can do safely'."

Here again is an explicit repudiation of one of the values we had identified — "can do" at any cost.

These were not mere words. The Air Force and the Defence Forces generally have made a series of organisational changes to give expression to these new priorities, some of which will be touched on in the next chapter. Moreover, the new policy has diffused throughout the Air Force. A manager of a remote Air Force facility, whom I met subsequently, told me that the focus on OHS had gone from 0% to 150%. In so saying, he was suggesting that the Air Force was now *too* committed to OHS. This is a criticism the Air Force can happily wear, for it is testimony to thoroughness with which the new policy is being implemented.

Chapter 10
Flying safety

In contrast to ground safety, discussed in Chapter 9, when it came to the safety of aircraft and their crews, the Royal Australian Air Force's performance was exemplary. On the whole, the organisational values described earlier did not have the potential to undermine safety in the air. The priority given to platforms in no way compromised the safety of aircrews — *their* safety was inextricably tied to the safety of their machines. Similarly, the priority of operations over logistics worked in favour of aircrews. Finally, the command and discipline system was far less a system of compulsion for the officers who flew the aircraft than it was for the fuel tank repair workers. Perhaps the major impediment to aircrew safety is their "can do" attitude, which results in pilots sometimes flying more sorties than is desirable with less than an adequate preparation.

The importance that the Air Force has assigned to flying safety has increased over time, as part of a society-wide growth of concern for safety. In addition, according to one inquiry witness, "there was a cultural shift ... in the early 1990s due to a number of accidents which caused management to look at how business was being done". In a two-year period to July 1992, there were 14 military aircraft crashes resulting in the loss of 23 lives. Perhaps the most shocking was the loss of a 707 and its five crew members when it crashed off the Victorian coast. Media coverage stimulated public concern, and the cultural shift in the Air Force was driven by this concern.

It is important to understand this background because it cautions against any assumption that the way in which "air safety" is managed can be transferred easily to "ground safety" management. Air safety had, and still has, a very high priority, in part because of the public visibility of aircraft crashes. In comparison, ground safety failures were less visible and were therefore less likely to be able to command the attention and resources which air safety enjoyed.

This contrasting approach to air and ground safety appears to be a feature of other flying organisations. There is evidence that while the major airlines have a flying safety record which is remarkably good by almost any standard, the employee injury rate is higher for the airline industry than for many other industries (Hudson, 2003). Among those at risk are baggage handlers and tarmac staff as well as flight attendants, who are sometimes hit by food carts, for example. While these latter injuries are incurred in the air, they have little to do with the safety of the aircraft and hence, it seems, are not well controlled. No doubt studies of commercial airlines would reveal many of the same processes at work as we discovered in this Australian Air Force inquiry.

The existence within the same organisation of two distinct cultures in relation to safety is what makes the Air Force such a fascinating case study. This chapter will examine how the Air Force made air safety a top priority; the examination will naturally highlight the ways it failed to make ground safety a priority.

The organisational context

It is a truism that safety is a line management responsibility. But many things compete for the attention of senior managers, and unless there are safety specialists within an organisation with sufficient status to command the attention of very senior managers, safety tends to fall by the wayside.

The Air Force implicitly recognised and continues to recognise this principle when it comes to air safety. One of the many agencies operating within the Defence Forces is the Directorate of Flying Safety. It is headed by a high ranking officer, a Group Captain, who has commanded a flying wing. This means that he can speak with authority to the pilots and their commanding officers. The prestige of this position reinforces the value of safety and the activities of his Directorate ensure that flying safety is always on the agenda.

There was no corresponding agency concerned with ground safety in the Air Force in 2001. After our inquiry began, a new Air Force Ground Safety Agency was created to fill the gap which had become obvious. However, it was headed by an acting Wing Commander, a significantly lower rank than that of the Director of Flying Safety. Moreover, the new head was an environmental health expert, with no experience commanding a maintenance wing. He had therefore to approach the commanding officers of maintenance wings, not as one of them, but to some extent as an outsider. In a sense his role was to inject occupational health and safety (OHS) concerns from the outside, while the Director of Flying Safety could develop them from within. This is a subtle but important distinction. It inadvertently reinforced the view that safety was an add-on when it came to maintenance, but integral when it came to flying.

The Board of Inquiry commented on this situation in its report and the Air Force responded by giving the Director of Flying Safety responsibility for ground safety as well. From this point of view, air and ground safety in the Air Force would henceforth have equivalent status. Defence itself set up a new agency, the Defence Workplace Safety Project, responsible for implementing the recommendations of the Board of Inquiry, and appointed as its head an engineering officer, also with the rank of Group Captain. Even more strikingly, perhaps, it created a new civilian organisation, an OHS Branch, the head of which was the equivalent of an Air Commodore, one level above a Group Captain. These organisational changes could be expected to keep ground safety far more in focus than previously.

The control of maintenance procedures

In order to achieve reliable aircraft operation, maintenance work must be of the highest possible standard and the Air Force has a special system to ensure the airworthiness of its aircraft.

The first principle of the system is to distinguish clearly between the design of maintenance processes and their execution. The design of processes is recognised as a specialist activity and is not done by those who carry out these processes. Maintenance processes are handed over to maintenance personnel to be carried out only when all potential engineering problems have been identified and rectified.

Second, the engineering design process is carefully managed and involves some or all of the following stages: initial design, design review, design approval, design acceptance, design implementation. These steps are carried out by different people and perhaps even different organisations. Approval is a critical step and the level at which approval takes place depends on the significance of the design.

Third, in order to ensure that the people or organisations carrying out these various steps are competent, they themselves must be approved or certified competent for their tasks.

This is a tried and true system which delivers high quality engineering outcomes and very high levels of aircraft safety.

The OHS aspects of the maintenance processes were not dealt with in this rigorous manner prior to the inquiry report. No distinction was made between the design and execution of maintenance processes from an OHS point of view. On the contrary, there was a general assumption that the teams responsible for carrying out the maintenance would acquire whatever personal protection equipment (PPE) was necessary to protect themselves and would iron out any problems which arose on the job. The production pressures referred to earlier meant that if no satisfactory PPE solutions existed, workers had to carry on regardless.

The airworthiness system described above would not work without an organisation specifically responsible for making it work. That organisation is the Directorate General of Technical Airworthiness. It is headed by an Air Commodore, who out-ranks all commanders of flying and maintenance wings. Among other things, the Directorate carries out audits of aircraft maintenance organisations to ensure that they are complying with the system described above, and audit reports are signed by the Director General himself. Because of the prestige of this agency, its audits are regarded as major events and audit findings are taken seriously. This is another example, then, of the way air safety has been built into the organisational structure of the Air Force.

At the time of our inquiry there was no corresponding agency responsible for OHS auditing, and OHS audits which did occur were carried out by non-commissioned officers within the maintenance organisation itself. Consequently, these audits did not have the same visibility or impact as audits done by the Directorate General of Technical Airworthiness.

Incident reporting

Safety in any large organisation depends on identifying information that things are in the process of going wrong, or may be about to go wrong, and acting on it. The aviation industry is well aware of this fact and has placed great emphasis on reporting systems. The Air Force is a model in this respect. It solicits reports of all incidents with potential consequences for air safety, describing them as aviation safety occurrence reports (ASORs). ASORs are made through the chain of command and are acted on by flying supervisors but are then passed on to the Directorate of Flying Safety for further comment and action if necessary. The Directorate produces a magazine called *Flying Feedback*, which publicises selected reports and the responses to them. This ensures that the ASOR system remains in the forefront of people's minds and is well used.

The Air Force has made great efforts to ensure that its ASOR system works, and pilots are schooled in the importance of making safety occurrence reports throughout their training. Reports are on a no-blame basis, and the effectiveness of the system can be gauged by the fact that reports are received of errors which pilots have made which were not witnessed by other people and which might therefore have been very easily covered up by the reporter. An example is instructive. A pilot discovered on landing that he had failed to arm his ejector seat at take off. This meant that he would not have been able to eject during flight, had he needed to. He reported his oversight. Other pilots came forward with similar reports and the Air Force was able to take remedial action.

Flying safety is not only affected by incidents which occur during flying operations. The violation of maintenance procedures, as well as other types of maintenance failures, impact on airworthiness and therefore on flying safety. Accordingly, the Directorate of Flying Safety introduced a second system — of Maintenance Aviation Safety Occurrence Reports (MASORs) — to collect information about such occurrences.

The Directorate took the view that violations of maintenance procedures were being driven by production pressures and a perceived need to get the job done at whatever cost. Nevertheless, it believed that one of the reasons these matters had gone unreported was the lack of any easy reporting mechanism. It argued, therefore, that the MASOR system had the potential to bring some of these issues to light and it now promotes the system vigorously through the pages of another publication called *Maintenance Feedback*. It should be stressed, however, that MASORs are about maintenance violations or occurrences that may threaten the safety of aircraft, not about occurrences that threaten the safety of maintenance workers.

Apart from ASORs and MASORs, there is also a so-called "incident" reporting system, operating within the Australian Defence Force generally, which functions almost exclusively as an injury reporting system. The kinds of symptoms experienced by fuel tank repair workers, such as memory loss, irritability or vertigo, were not commonly viewed as incidents and so were not reported as such. The focus on traumatic injury is well captured in the following comment made by one supervisor in answer to a question about incident reporting:

> "I don't think we had any incidents of our equipment suddenly becoming dangerous or anything like that. Health-wise I believe we only had the one incident of a chap that was affected by fumes from the air conditioning hose being partially disconnected, but actual incidents — we had no accidents and I think I should point that out right now (Clarkson, Hopkins and Taylor, 2001:5-1)."

The supervisor could not recall whether an incident form had been filled out in the case of the man overcome by fumes but he did say such a report would not have come from the fuel tank repair section; if anyone had made a report it would have been the medical section to which the man had been sent, he said. (The medical section did not, in fact, make such reports.) Other supervisors gave evidence that to their knowledge there had never been an occasion to fill out an incident report in the fuel tank repair section.

Incident reporting systems are not, in principle, restricted to incidents which cause harm; they are usually intended to include incidents which have the *potential* to cause harm — dangerous occurrences or near misses. In practice, however, the Defence incident report system tends not to be used in this way. Incidents concerning the use of personal protective equipment (PPE) are particularly unlikely to be reported. For instance, the fact that gloves disintegrated within five minutes of contact with chemicals was never made the subject of an incident report at Amberley. Nor was it ever reported that workers were at times unable to wear respirators or goggles because they got in the way and interfered with the job.

It is instructive to compare some of the aviation safety occurrences reported through the ASOR system with occurrences in the fuel tank repair section. On one occasion, a Hornet pilot experienced five seconds of starred vision in level flight and some time later feelings of nausea and mild stomach ache. The symptoms gradually worsened and he returned to base and was removed by ambulance to the medical section. The plane then underwent a maintenance examination which failed to reveal any anomalies. However, the oxygen converter was replaced as a precaution. Subsequent investigation linked the incident to viral gastroenteritis rather than a cockpit environment cause.

As for the fuel tank repair section, there were various occasions described to the Board when workers felt dizzy or close to passing out while inside tanks. Passing out inside a fuel tank in a toxic atmosphere is potentially fatal; the current emphasis on confined space entry training, both inside and outside the Defence Forces, has come about precisely because of a number of such fatalities. Clearly, feeling dizzy in a fuel tank is no less dangerous to the person than feeling dizzy in a cockpit, yet these occurrences went unreported and failed to generate any investigation or remedial action.

A second comparison concerns problems that Blackhawk helicopter loadmasters experienced with hearing protection. The Directorate of Flying Safety received 23 such reports. Loadmasters wearing double hearing protection were unable to hear radio instructions from other crew members and several of these incidents resulted in the cancellation of the sortie. Various solutions were tried and the problem was finally fixed with a new helmet and a special communications ear piece.

In these loadmaster cases, PPE interfered with the job, in much the same way that respirators and goggles sometimes interfered with the ability of fuel tank workers to carry out their activities in very confined spaces. However, rather than expecting loadmasters to remove the equipment so as to get on with the job, as supervisors expected fuel tank workers to do, commanders cancelled the jobs and filled out ASORs. Eventually, a proper solution was found.

It is clear that an incident or occurrence reporting system could easily be used to report problems being experienced with PPE as well as health symptoms of the type suffered by fuel tank repair workers. Had such a system been working effectively, the problems in the fuel tank repair section would have come to light much earlier than they did. The absence of a functioning reporting system for maintenance workers is symptomatic of the relative lack of concern for ground safety.

Making a reporting system work is about creating a culture of reporting; that is, an environment in which reporting is an ongoing practice and not simply a theoretical possibility. But creating a culture of reporting requires continuous effort. The Air Force had put this effort into making its ASOR system work, but not into creating a culture of reporting among its maintenance workers.

The Board was given an interesting example of how the Navy is trying to create a culture of reporting. The Navy became aware that one of its vessels had a high rate of reporting relative to a comparable vessel. Rather than querying the high reporting vessel, the issue was raised with the commanding officer of the under-reporting ship and within a few months its incident reporting rate had risen. This is the kind of intervention which is necessary to make reporting systems work. Ironically, it is the low number of incident reports which constitutes poor performance in this context.

To return to the Air Force, it was an organisation committed to air safety, with a variety of practices aimed at achieving this outcome. However, there were no comparable practices aimed at ensuring ground safety. The comparison is an illuminating one for it demonstrates just what is necessary to create a culture of safety.

Chapter 11

The Royal Australian Air Force: concluding thoughts

Culture as organisational practices

The preceding chapters have identified a number of Air Force values as contributing to the profound differences in approach to air and ground safety. As noted in Part A of this book, values can be inferred from the organisational practices to which they give rise; we discern the values by observing the practices. The commitment to air safety was demonstrated, for instance, by the aviation safety reporting practices and the rigorous practices of maintenance design and authorisation. There were no similar practices in relation to ground safety.

Furthermore, practices are entirely within the control of management, if it devotes sufficient attention to embedding the practices it wants. The Air Force culture was a direct reflection of what its leadership attended to and overtly valued.

Interestingly, there was one aspect of the behaviour of maintenance workers to which the leadership had attended and where a profound culture change had been the result. The issue was the way in which maintenance workers treated the D6AC steel used in the F111 airframe. This steel is ultra high strength, but as a result, it is extremely sensitive to scratching. Failure to treat it carefully can result in catastrophic failure in flight. Several USAF F111s crashed in the 1960s and 1970s for this reason. According to the Director General of Technical Airworthiness:

> "All this demanded high standards of attention to detail and personal care by technicians working with it, including constant coverage with protective barriers. Before working with D6AC steel, all staff were trained in special maintenance requirements. During maintenance, there was constant reinforcement and swift supervisory action in the event of any variation to, or abrogation of authorised procedures. Hence, I recall at the time an extremely high degree of overall awareness of special requirements which, as long as the basis for the requirement was clearly explained and understood by staff, led to high standards of compliance. In turn, staff showed a great deal of pride in feeling well informed and working with this new technology (Clarkson, Hopkins and Taylor, 2001:5-6)."

The Director General is describing here an intense campaign to change the culture of the workforce in relation to the handling of this special steel. It was clearly a campaign motivated by a concern about air safety; there was no similar campaign in relation to ground safety.

What is especially interesting about this example is that it was a campaign to change the culture of *maintenance* workers. It shows that, contrary to some suggestions, the culture of this group can be changed. All that is required is the close attention of leadership.

Culture and organisational structure

Part C has shown how the culture of an organisation is influenced by the very structure of the organisation. In a large organisation like the Air Force, cultural themes such as safety are only likely to be prominent if the organisation has agencies within it that have specific responsibility for these matters. The better resourced these agencies are, and the higher the status of their heads, the more prominent are those themes.

Two agencies, in particular, ensured that air safety had the highest priority. One of these focused on the activities of the aviators themselves, the Directorate of Flying Safety; and the other, on the mechanical safety of aircraft, the Directorate General of Technical Airworthiness. As noted earlier, these organisations were headed by senior officers, one, a Group Captain, and the other, an even higher status officer, an Air Commodore. These people did not have safety as one of their responsibilities; it was their exclusive focus. In structuring itself in this way the Air Force ensured that air safety would be effectively championed at a senior level and that a culture of air safety would be effectively promoted.

As we saw, there was no corresponding agency or leader responsible for ground safety. It was therefore to be expected that ground safety would have a low priority. Viewed in this light, the Air Force failure to protect its maintenance workers from toxic chemicals is no surprise. The failure was an outcome of the way the Air Force was organised.

This analysis suggests a way forward for organisations wishing to promote a culture of safety. They must set up organisational nodes that promote such a culture. These nodes must be powerful enough to dictate what happens at the work site. Culture is about practices and organisations must be structured in such a way as to guarantee the practices they want.

Outside influences

As in the Glenbrook case study (Part B), it must be recognised that the Air Force is not isolated from the wider society. A number of external factors influenced the internal processes and outcomes identified here. I have already noted one — greater public concern about air crashes than about other health and safety issues — leading to a greater emphasis within the Air Force on air safety.

A second external factor which has been touched on but deserves greater emphasis was the government-initiated cost-cutting and down-sizing which had been going on in the Air Force. This contributed to the lack of engineering supervision available to maintenance workers and the relative isolation in which they worked. Moreover, the under-funding of Air Force medical services contributed to the failure to diagnose the problems being experienced by maintenance workers.

Tragically, the culture of medicine itself was also a contributing factor. To understand how this happened I need to backtrack a little. A year before matters came to a head and the final program was cancelled, maintenance workers had complained to the Amberley medical centre about their symptoms — loss of memory and so on. The medical centre organised some blood tests. The tests failed to identify any abnormalities, and workers were told: "on the basis of these results, it can be concluded that current protective measures used in the fuel tank repair section are adequate for the prevention of overexposure to chemical hazards". This was a particularly unfortunate conclusion because the tests turned out later to be largely inappropriate.

Why was the medical centre so ready to give priority to the blood test results and to dismiss the reported symptoms in this way? To answer this question requires a digression on medical thinking. A distinction is made in the medical profession between symptoms and signs. Symptoms are those matters of which patients complain; signs are the indications of pathology which are visible or detectable to the medical practitioner. Thus a headache is a symptom but not a sign; an abnormal blood test result may be a sign but not a symptom. An indicator such as a skin rash is both a symptom and a sign.

There is a general tendency in the medical community to give preference to signs when seeking to diagnose problems (Engel, 1981). From the point of view of the medical observer, signs are objective; reports of symptoms which are not detectable to the medical observer tend to be viewed as less reliable. From the point of view of the patient, the situation is almost the reverse. The symptoms are the objective reality, and signs, such as blood test results, are indirect and abstract.

Medicine faces a dilemma when patients complain of symptoms but there are no signs available to medical observers. There is a risk in these circumstances that medical observers will dismiss the symptoms. This was precisely what happened at Amberley. The outcome was that exposure of maintenance workers to toxic chemicals was prolonged by an aspect of medical culture over which the Air Force had no control.

It is important to identify external influences which contributed to the outcome for at least two reasons. First, it is easy to blame organisations when tragedies of this nature occur. But blaming an organisation after the event is seldom helpful. Understanding the context in which the organisation operates reduces this tendency. Second, significant organisational change may depend on changing the context in some way. Given that the focus on air safety has been driven in part by public pressure, it may be difficult for the Air Force to achieve the same high standards for ground safety until there is equivalent public concern about safety on the hangar floor.

The causes of the exposure

The Board of Inquiry produced a diagram identifying the network of causes which it had identified as contributing to the damage done to the health of Air Force maintenance workers (see Fig 2). The diagram is constructed according to the logic outlined at the end of Part B of this book. Not all the causes identified on the diagram have been discussed here and the reader wanting a more detailed discussion is referred to the Board's report. The diagram is arranged in five layers, one of which is Air Force values. All the values represented at this level are discussed in this book.

Figure 2: Causes of health damage to Air Force workers

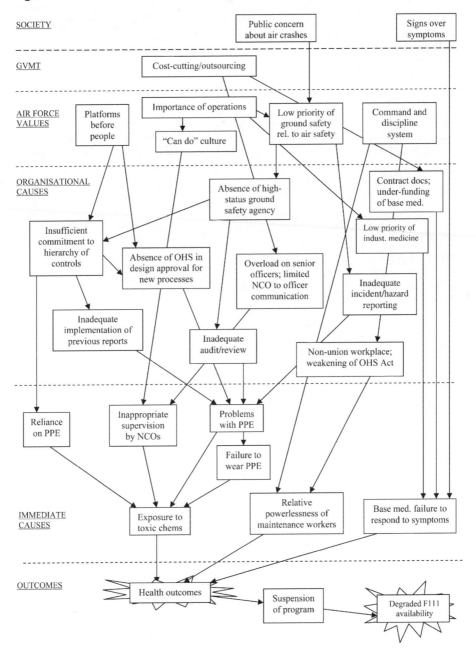

part D

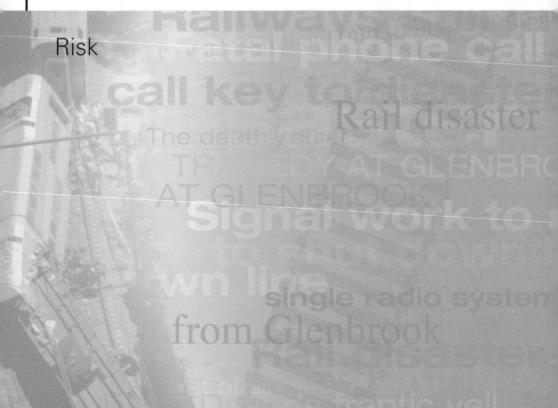

Risk

Chapter 12

Quantitative risk assessment and acceptable risk: a critique

The aim of risk management is to identify and reduce risks. But, how far do managers need to go in reducing the level of risk? How low is low enough?

The law provides one answer to this question. Risks must be reduced "so far as is reasonably practicable".[1] A great deal has been written about what this means, and although no clear cut criteria have emerged, there is general agreement about what needs to be considered (Johnstone, 1997:202-217). One consideration is the severity of the risk: how serious are the possible consequences? Another is the question of foreseeability: would a reasonable employer[2] have been able to foresee what might happen? A third consideration is whether means are available to control the risk, and a fourth is whether the cost of installing these controls is justified in the circumstances. According to one influential view (quoted in HSE, 2001:62), if there is a "gross disproportion" between the cost of the precautions and the level of risk, that is, if the risk is insignificant in relation to the financial sacrifice involved in rectifying it, a reasonable employer is not bound to take the precautions in question.

These considerations do not generate a set of rules which can be automatically applied to determine whether the risk is as low as is reasonably practicable, and ultimately a judgment must be made in each situation about what a reasonable employer would do. Such judgments are to some extent subjective, which is not to say that they are arbitrary. One guide which courts use as to what is reasonably practicable is current good practice in the industry (Brooks, 1993:82). Employers who fail to comply with current good practice are likely to be found not to have done what was reasonably practicable, should the issue arise. One implication of this is that what is reasonably practicable will vary, from industry to industry, and over time, as industry standards improve. It is not a concept which can ever be given a fixed meaning.

---

1   See for example, the United Kingdom's *Health and Safety at Work Act 1974* sec 2(1). In the state of Victoria, risks must be reduced "so far as is practicable", but the way this is defined makes it clear that there is no significant difference between the two tests.

2   It is not only employers who have a duty of care, but for ease of exposition at this point, I shall use the term employer rather than the more accurate but more cumbersome term, duty-holder.

Anglo-Saxon law is content with this approach. There is a general assumption in the common law that inflexible principles cannot be laid down in advance, that human circumstances are too varied and complex to be reducible to any formula, that each case has to be considered on its merits, and that the law evolves as a result of case by case decision making. Only after a series of cases has been decided can general principles be discerned, but these are always provisional and subject to modification as new cases arise.

On the other hand, Western civilisation is characterised by a drive for consistency and systematisation (Bendix, 1966), and from this perspective, the common law approach to deciding what level of risk is low enough, appears unacceptably arbitrary and subjective. Hence the trend towards quantitative risk assessment (QRA). The premise of QRA is that if levels of risk can be estimated numerically, we can specify an acceptable upper limit and require managers to drive risk below this level. Provided the determination of the acceptable numerical level is agreed beforehand and is based on some coherent reasoning, this is presumed to be a more objective and hence more satisfactory way of deciding how low is low enough. This thinking has emerged in industries such as nuclear power, petroleum production, and railways, and is driven, in part, by regulators seeking objective ways of justifying their demands that companies carry out further risk reduction activities.[3]

It is, however, intuitively obvious that where risk is being imposed on workers or members of the public, the concept of acceptable risk is contentious. "Acceptable to whom?" we are entitled to ask. Moreover, to say in some context that a risk is acceptable is to say that it is not worth spending money to further reduce it. Thus the notion of acceptable risk carries with it an implicit notion of the value of a human life, again an obviously contentious idea. Quantitative risk assessment therefore poses profound moral dilemmas, as well as a variety of other conceptual and practical problems. The aim of this chapter is to examine some of these problems as they have emerged in current attempts to apply the QRA framework.

Before moving on, it should be recognised that the moral dilemmas which confront the proponents of QRA are inherent in the legal approach as well. But they remain dilemmas which are never finally resolved. QRA, on the other hand, purports to resolve the dilemmas by developing objective criteria to decide whether risks are low enough. This apparent claim to objectivity amounts to a denial of dilemma and contributes to the controversy about QRA.

---

3   The emergence of QRA was endorsed in the Cullen report (1990) into the fire on the Piper Alpha platform in the North Sea.

Objective and subjective risk

QRA is built on the assumption that risk can be objectively measured. This is often associated with a second assumption, which is that if subjective perceptions of risk do not coincide with the objective measures, the subjective perceptions must be wrong.

These assumptions are thoroughly problematic. Subjective perceptions are not just imperfect estimates of an objective reality. They exist independently of measured risk and may indeed influence it. Consider this, for example. The road accident fatality rate for children has steadily declined in the United Kingdom, leading some observers to conclude that the roads are safer for children than they used to be. However, half of all children killed on the roads are pedestrians (BMA, 1990), and one reason for the drop in the fatality rate is that parents have become increasingly concerned about their children being hit by cars. Adams (1995:12,13) notes that "in 1971, for example, 80% of seven and eight year old children in England travelled to school on their own, unaccompanied by an adult. By 1990 this figure had dropped to 9%; the questionnaire survey disclosed that the parent's main reason for not allowing their children to travel independently was fear of traffic". The growing perception that roads were dangerous places had altered behaviour in such a way as to reduce the measured fatality rate.

Pedestrian road crossings provide an interesting example of the effect of risk perception. Casual observation suggests that pedestrians are less likely to be on the lookout for oncoming traffic when they step out onto a pedestrian crossing than when they step out to cross a road at some other point. Some pedestrians seem almost oblivious to the possibility that a car may fail to stop at a crossing. If it turned out that, by some measure, the number of pedestrians hit by cars on crossings was disproportionately high, we would be unlikely to conclude that using pedestrian crossings was objectively riskier than crossing at unmarked locations. Rather, we would conclude that the reason for the disproportionate number of accidents at crossings was that pedestrians at crossings were tending to drop their guard.

Adams describes another important way in which risk perceptions can influence objective risk indicators. He outlines a theory of risk compensation, which assumes that everyone has a level of risk-taking behaviour with which they are comfortable and that this varies from one individual to another (1995:14-16). One consequence of this is that if the authorities reduce the risk to which we are exposed, we may adjust our behaviour to restore the level of risk at which we are comfortable.

Consider the following. Many drivers travel on country roads as fast as, in their judgment, the road allows. If a government attempts to make such a road safer by widening it and straightening out the worst bends — removing the black spots — most drivers respond by driving faster, as fast as, in their view, the improved road allows. Quite possibly in these circumstances the accident rate will not decrease, and the fatality rate may even increase because, with cars travelling at higher speed, the proportion of accidents that result in fatalities is likely to increase. Driver perceptions are that this is now a safer road, which no doubt it is, controlling for speed, but those very perceptions increase the risk of fatality.

This discussion demonstrates that objective or measured risk is strongly influenced by our perceptions and that the relationship may be surprisingly complex. Accident rates may be low because the perceived risk is high and conversely, rates may increase because the perceived risk has declined.[4]

Risk and rate

The preceding discussion demonstrates a second, quite intriguing aspect of the relationship between objective and subjective risk; namely, that our willingness to interpret fatality *rates* as indicators of *risk* is substantially affected by our perception of the intrinsic risk of the activity. No-one seriously believes that roads are safer places for children to play on or near, simply because accident rates have gone down. Moreover, we believe that crossing a road at a pedestrian crossing is intrinsically safer than crossing elsewhere, regardless of what the statistics might show.

The situation is nicely illustrated by an Australian study of the risks associated with a number of activities, including football (Higson, 1989:9). Using estimated player populations as its denominator, it found that the fatality rate per million person-years for rugby union and league combined was 29, while the corresponding figure for touch football was 37. Touch football prohibits tackling, yet, on the numbers, it is a riskier activity than rugby. This flies in the face of reason. We all "know" that rugby is intrinsically riskier than touch football and this is a case where we are not prepared to accept the objective rates as indicators of intrinsic risk. The author of the study offered no explanation for this anomaly, but we can certainly imagine one. Touch football attracts players who may be quite unfit and disproportionately likely to suffer fatal heart attacks on the field. Such a possibility would enable us to make sense of the apparently higher risk involved in what we believe to be an intrinsically safer activity.[5] Risk, then, is not another word for rate. We can accept that the fatality rate for touch football may be higher than the rate for rugby, and then set about explaining why. However, we are unlikely to accept that touch football is a riskier activity than rugby.

---

4   A more complete discussion of the problematic nature of objective risk can be found in
     Pidgeon et al, 1992:94-97.

5   Another possible explanation is that the difference is not statistically significant.

A further reason for distinguishing between risk and rate is that risk is always highly dependent on the specific situation. For instance, the death rate from lightening strike is less than one person per million per annum.[6] If this is taken as an indicator of risk, we conclude that the risk of death by lightening strike is insignificant. On a clear day, that is unarguable, but if one is caught in a violent electrical storm, it is surely prudent to take reasonable risk reduction measures; for example, by staying in the open and not seeking shelter under a tree. The overall rate is no guide to the risk we face in these circumstances.

The meaning and relevance of the concepts of risk and rate depend to some extent on one's vantage point. Suppose we are talking about an insurance company which has insured car owners against accidents. It needs to know the overall accident rate so that it can set its premiums in such a way as to cover all claims and stay in business. For the insurance company, risk of accident and accident rate mean much the same thing.[7] Moreover, if it charges all drivers the same premium, this is simply an expedient way of covering the financial risk to which it is exposed and involves no assumption that all drivers are equally at risk of having an accident. As far as the company is concerned, the real risk which any individual faces is irrelevant. If the company's data allow it to identify groups, for example, age groups or gender groups, whose accident rates differ systematically, it may decide to offer different premiums to different groups; but again, these premiums will be set in accordance with the overall accident rate of the group and without any presumption that this is the actual risk faced by any particular individual in the group.

From the point of view of the individual driver, however, it is the accident rates which are irrelevant, since they provide no indication of the risk inherent in any particular situation. That will depend on all the circumstances and is quite unknowable in any quantitative sense. That is not to say that there is nothing we can do as individual drivers to reduce the risks we face. Various risk reduction strategies are available to us, such as driving more slowly around corners. We may not be able to quantify the effectiveness of these strategies but we know by a priori reasoning that they will reduce the risk we face. In short, although the level of risk involved in any such course of action cannot be known numerically, we quite reasonably make qualitative estimates and act accordingly.

The preceding discussion has demonstrated that it is often necessary to distinguish between risk and rate. Rates are measurable; risks often are not. The result is that, in many contexts, quantitative risk assessment is almost a contradiction in terms!

---

6   A calculation in the United Kingdom puts the figure at 1 person in 18.7 million people (HSE, 2001:70).

7   The financial risk is different.

Determining numerical risk limits

The risk of fatality is often expressed as a ratio, for example one in 10^4, or an equivalent rate, 10^{-4} (0.0001), in both cases, per annum. What this means, in this example, is that on average we expect one fatality per year for every 10,000 exposed individuals. What rate, then, is acceptable?

A recent article by Swiss authors Flüeler and Seiler (2003) provides an elegant and reasonably coherent answer to this question, which I shall take as representative of thinking on this matter.

They propose two rules. The first is that there be an absolute upper limit on the risk to which individuals are to be exposed. Anything above this is intolerable from a moral point of view and cannot be justified, no matter what societal advantage there may be in exceeding this limit. Second, risk should be reduced as far below this absolute limit as is cost effective. Whereas the first rule is morally based, the second is based on utilitarian considerations: risk reduction is required only if it is judged to be financially justified. I shall say about more about this later.

So, what is the limit beyond which it is morally intolerable to impose risk? Flüeler and Seiler argue that it varies for different categories of risk and they identify four such categories:

Category 1: voluntary risk exposure in order to satisfy one's own desires, eg dangerous sports;

Category 2: high degree of choice involving direct individual benefit, eg car driving;

Category 3: low degree of choice, individual benefit, eg working conditions; and

Category 4: involuntary, imposed risk, no direct benefit, eg dangerous installation located in neighbourhood.

These categories vary in the extent to which the victim is responsible for his or her own exposure: at one extreme participants in dangerous sports such as rock climbing are entirely responsible for their own exposure; at the other extreme, if the authorities choose to locate a nuclear power station in one's neighbourhood, there is little one can do about the risk, short of selling up and moving away. Flüeler and Seiler nominate limits ranging from 10^{-3} to 10^{-5} as being appropriate.[8] For a risk which is totally imposed and provides no direct benefit for the exposed person, category 4 risks, the limit of tolerability is 1 death in 100,000 (10^{-5}); while for category 2 risks, such as car driving, the limit of tolerability is 1 death in 1000 (10^{-3}). They suggest it may be inappropriate to specify any risk level as intolerable for people who voluntarily engage in

---

8   Unless otherwise indicated, risks are per annum.

dangerous sports. To do so, it could be argued, would be an unwarranted interference with freedom of choice.

Flüeler and Seiler suggest that the limits of tolerability which they specify are based on normative or value judgments, but they also claim that these judgments are guided by empirical considerations, in the following ways. First, their proposed limits correspond roughly to the actual risk levels in their own country, Switzerland. In a sense, these are the rates which Swiss society already accepts. Second, the limits of tolerability are in part set by reference to the overall risk of death to which we are subject from all sources, including disease. The age group with the lowest death rate per annum from all causes is 10 to 15 year olds; their death rate is about 1 in 10,000 (10^{-4}). For adults in the prime of life, the death rate is more like 1 in 1000 (10^{-3}), (HSE, 2001:69; Tweeddale, 2003:71). Flüeler and Seiler argue that the imposed risk is acceptable as long as it is small in relation to overall risk of death. As they put it, "the philosophy requires not to unduly increase this natural lethal risk by technical risks" (2003:218). From this they derive the limit of 10^{-5} per year for imposed risk, the logic being that this is an order of magnitude lower than the lowest age-specific death rate. The rate 10^{-5} is thus a baseline, appropriate for imposed risks, and higher levels of risk are tolerable to the extent that the activity involves an element of choice. The authors do not, however, provide any way of quantifying the degree of voluntariness or associating the degree of voluntariness with the acceptable numerical risk level, so the levels they propose remain somewhat arbitrary.

This style of thinking has been given an authoritative stamp by the occupational health and safety (OHS) regulator in the United Kingdom, the Health and Safety Executive (HSE), which has produced an influential document, *Reducing Risks, Protecting People*. However, whereas Flüeler and Seiler have essentially only two levels of risk, tolerable and intolerable, the HSE has three: intolerable, tolerable and acceptable. See Figure 3.

Figure 3: HSE framework for the tolerability of risk

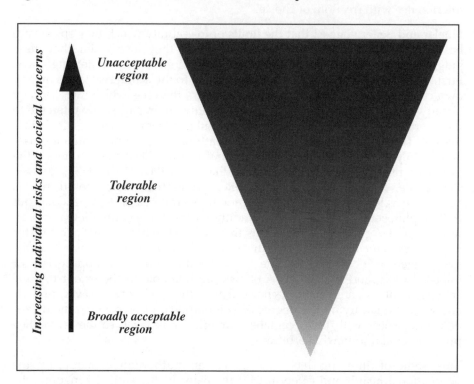

At the highest level, if a risk is deemed intolerable, the activity is ruled out, unless a way can be found to reduce it to the point that it falls into one of the lower levels.

Within the tolerable region, risks must be assessed and controlled, so far as reasonably practicable; which is to say, efforts must be made to reduce them as long as the cost of those efforts is not grossly disproportionate to the benefits. This is precisely the legal test discussed above, but it is referred to in the HSE document as the ALARP principle — as low as reasonably practicable.

At the bottom of the scale is the broadly acceptable region. According to the HSE, "risks falling into this region are generally regarded as insignificant and adequately controlled. ... The levels of risk characterising this region are comparable to those that people regard as insignificant or trivial in their daily lives" (2001:43). This comment would suggest that risks in this region can be ignored. The HSE says explicitly that "we, as regulators, would not usually require further action to reduce [such] risks", but they go on immediately to say, "unless reasonably practicable measures are available".

There is a paradox associated with this last statement. The law requires that risks be reduced as far as reasonably practicable, regardless of the starting point, and it is therefore appropriate for the HSE to note that even in the region of acceptability, employers should aim for further risk reductions if it is reasonably practicable to do so. But if that is the case, there is no real distinction between the regions of tolerability and acceptability; in both cases, risks are to be kept as low as reasonably practicable.

How is this paradox to be resolved by those seeking to follow the HSE framework? One obvious way is simply to ignore the ALARP requirement for the lowest risk category — acceptable risks. Proceeding in this way maintains the rationale of the three layered approach: intolerable risks must be reduced at all costs; tolerable risks should be reduced if reasonably practicable; acceptable risks require no further action. This is indeed how some companies have interpreted the framework. Figure 4 is an attempt by one major oil company to adapt the HSE framework for one of its offshore production platforms. It describes the region of tolerability as the ALARP region and it interprets broadly acceptable risk as requiring no further risk reduction.

Figure 4: Offshore individual risk criteria

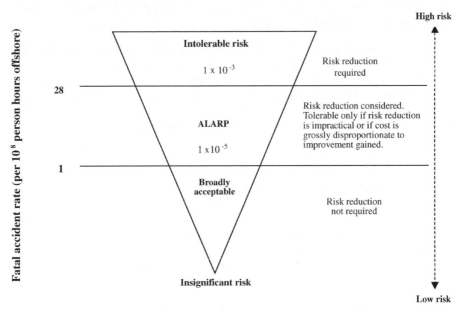

The following example demonstrates this approach in action. A company with offshore petroleum production platforms had reduced the risk to its employees to the region of acceptability. It decided it wished to install another gas compressor on one of its platforms. Compressors bring with them an increased risk of fire, and risk engineers calculated that the installation of the compressor would increase the total risk to which employees on this platform were exposed to a level above the company's stated goal for its employees. It turns out that the greatest risk to offshore production workers is the helicopter flights to and from the platform. Risk engineers therefore concluded that by altering the shift arrangement so as to reduce the number of helicopter flights to which workers were exposed they could bring the total risk exposure back to below the acceptable limit.

The problem is that if it was reasonably practicable to reduce the number of helicopter flights after the installation of the compressor, it must have been reasonably practicable to do so beforehand. The company had not considered doing so because the risk was already acceptably low. One would have to conclude that prior to the installation of the compressor, the company had failed to reduce the risk to its employees as far as reasonably practicable. For this company, as for the company which drew up Figure 4, ALARP did not apply where risks were below a certain level. In principle, therefore, these companies are at odds with the law.

I turn now to the numerical thresholds of these different regions of risk. The HSE argues that 1 in 1 million (10^{-6}) is extremely low, in relation to the death rate for any age group in the whole population, and should be regarded as acceptable for workers and public alike. It will be noticed in Figure 4 that the petroleum company has set the threshold of acceptability at 10^{-5}. The difference is probably not of much practical significance.

As for the other end of the risk spectrum, here is what the HSE has to say about the limits of tolerability:

> "An individual risk of death of 1 in 1000 per annum should on its own represent the dividing line between what could be just tolerable for any substantial group of workers for any large part of a working life, and what is unacceptable for any but fairly exceptional groups. For members of the public who have a risk imposed on them "in the wider interest of society", this limit is judged to be an order of magnitude lower — at 1 in 10,000 per annum (HSE, 2001:46)."

In Figure 4 it can be seen that the petroleum company concerned accepts the figure of 1 in 1000 as its limit of tolerability.

The HSE statement raises a number of issues. First, it acknowledges that for some "exceptional groups" of workers, the tolerable level of risk may be higher than 1 in 1000. This seriously undermines the significance of the limit as a guideline. Consider the risk to helicopter pilots and crop dusting pilots to name just two high-risk occupations. The risk to such groups may well be considerably above 1 in 1000 per annum. Should regulators regard this situation as intolerable and demand that the risk be reduced no matter what the cost, or should they regard these occupational groups as "exceptional" and their risk exposure as therefore tolerable? The tolerability framework provides no guidance.

It is worth noting that the legal framework is not bedevilled by this problem. The law does not regard any particular level of risk as intolerable on a priori grounds. Provided risks have been reduced as low as reasonably practicable, even very high-risk levels may be justified. Enormous efforts have been made to reduce the risks of helicopter flights to offshore petroleum platforms in the United Kingdom, and it is arguable that the risk to these pilots is now as low as is reasonably practicable, but it would be foolish to suggest that there are not more steps that could reasonably be taken to reduce the risks to crop dusting pilots in Australia.

A second issue is raised by the HSE proposal to use different limits for workers and members of the public on whom risks are imposed. Flüeler and Seiler made the same distinction. The presumption is that workers exercise some choice about where they work and their risk exposure is therefore to some extent voluntary. On this basis, a higher level of risk is tolerable. It should be noted, however, that for many workers the choice is between manual work, with all its attendant risks, and unemployment. Most such workers do not have the option of retreating to the relative safety of white collar jobs. That being so, it is somewhat unrealistic to treat workplace risk as voluntarily assumed.

There is also a question of equity here. For most groups of workers, and especially white collar and service workers, the risk of death at work is orders of magnitude below 1 in 1000 per annum. In the service industry in the United Kingdom, for instance, it is 1 in 333,000. The risk to construction workers, on the other hand, is 1 in 17,000, and in "mining and quarrying of energy producing materials", the risk is 1 in 9000 (HSE, 2001:70). To conclude that the risk to these manual workers is tolerable because it is less than 1 in 1000 is, in effect, to endorse the unequal distribution of risks across the workforce.

The distinction between workers and other members of the public which is built into the acceptable/tolerable risk framework turns out to be quite problematic in some contexts. Consider its application in the railways, for example. The safety case which was prepared by the United Kingdom's Railtrack corporation lays out the tolerable levels of risk for different categories of stakeholders (Railtrack, 1999:22). For employees, the limit is 1 in 1000. For individual members of the public adjacent to the track for any reason, for example, at level crossings, the tolerable risk drops to 1 in 10,000. This is presumably justified on the grounds that for such people the risk is imposed, rather than being in any sense voluntarily assumed. The largest stakeholder group consists of passengers, especially commuters going to and from work. Railtrack judges the limit of tolerability for this group to be 1 in 10,000, ten times less than the figure for employees. No clear justification is provided for this distinction. Passengers are in some respects members of the public in a way that employees are not. But, the justification which the HSE proposes for a lower level of tolerability for certain members of the public is not that they are members of the public, but that the risks concerned have been imposed on them. Rail commuters do not have risks imposed on them in the way that householders do if a nuclear power station is built in their neighbourhood. On the contrary, they take steps daily to put themselves at risk by boarding trains to go to work. In this way they are no different from employees who daily put themselves at risk by being at work. The point is that *going* to work is no more voluntary or involuntary than *being* at work.[9] If that is accepted, there can be no justification for tolerating a higher level of risk for rail employees than for rail passengers.

Although Railtrack cites the HSE discussion on tolerability of risk, it does not in fact justify its tolerability limits by reference to the degree of choice which individuals exercise in assuming the risk. Rather, its limits are determined by reference to the existing accident rates of these groups. The argument appears to be that, because rail employees are killed at a higher rate than passengers, this difference must be tolerable. Used in this way, the idea of tolerability simply serves to legitimate the status quo.

Acceptable to whom?

The notion of tolerability or acceptability immediately raises the question of tolerable or acceptable to whom? The answer, frequently, is "society". As the HSE says, tolerable refers to "a willingness by society as a whole to live with a risk so as to secure certain benefits ..." (2001:8). But this is to confuse the way things are with the way things ought to be. In one sense, of course, the fact that things are as they are means that we are currently tolerating them, as a matter of fact. However, tolerability is more fundamentally a normative concept. The crucial question is — *should* things be as they are, or should they be regarded as intolerable? This question cannot be answered by reference to the existing state of affairs.

A further problem with this whole approach is that it personifies society in an inappropriate way. Societies don't have views; individuals do. And the views of individuals may differ depending on whether or not they are exposed to the risk. While the shareholders in a company may find that a risk of one fatality per 1000 workers per year is tolerable, the workers concerned may not.

---

9   Indeed, workers compensation law has often regarded the journey to work as *part* of the
     day's work.

One solution to this problem is to speak not of tolerable or acceptable risks, but rather, of approved risk. This is the risk that the regulators or legislators accept for an activity or occupation. This is a relatively unambiguous term, in that it is clear who is doing the approving, and there is no implication that the risk is necessarily acceptable to those exposed to it. Tweeddale argues that were such a term to be widely adopted it would make the discussion of the limits of risk less "provocative and paternalistic" (2003:70).

The acceptability of multiple fatalities

The public reaction when numbers of people are killed in a single event, such as a mine explosion or an aircraft crash, is often far more intense than when the same number die in separate events; for example, in separate car crashes. Risk analysts conclude that because the risks associated with multiple fatalities give rise to particular societal concerns, they must be treated differently. Putting this another way, the acceptable risk of death for an individual is lower if the individual dies along with others than if he or she is the only one killed. Specifically, the death of 10 people in one accident is 100 times less acceptable than the death of a single person; the death of 100 people is 10,000 times less acceptable than the death of a single person, and so on (Tweeddale, 2003:73,83; R2A, 2002:4.4).

There is something very disturbing about these attempts to relate acceptability to the number of fatalities. For those who die, as for their loved ones, it makes no difference whether they are killed alone or with others.

Despite these reservations, policy makers in the United Kingdom have, very tentatively, proposed a limit of this kind for the risk associated with allowing a major chemical plant to continue operation adjacent to a housing estate.

> "In such circumstances, HSE proposes that the risk of an accident causing the death of 50 people or more in a single event should be regarded as intolerable if the frequency is estimated to be more than 1 in 5000 per annum (HSE, 2001:47)."

The HSE notes that such thinking may not apply to "very different types of risk such as flooding from a burst dam or crushing from crowds in sports stadia". Tweeddale makes the point dramatically by reference to the barrier on the river Thames in London:

> "At times of unusually high tide, if the wind is blowing strongly from the east, the level of the sea in the Thames estuary rises substantially, with the potential to flood large areas of London. Because of long-term, gradual subsidence of the land, the risk of this has been assessed as very high, perhaps as much as around 1 in 50 years. So a barrier was built, able to be raised from the bed of the river at the onset of such times. It is estimated that this barrier or the surrounding high ground could now be

flooded with a risk of around 1 in 1000 per year. This is clearly a major improvement. But it is estimated that, in the event of the barrier being overtopped, hundreds of people would drown, in spite of all the emergency procedures that might be taken. Thus, this installation is not able to reduce the risks from the natural hazard of flooding to a level meeting typical industrial society risk criteria (2003:84)."

Tweeddale's last point can be seen by comparing the Thames barrier risk with the HSE proposal. For industrial installations, the risk of an event which causes 50 deaths is tolerable only if it is less than 1 in 5000 per annum; the tolerable risk of an event causing *hundreds* of deaths would be much lower. On the other hand, the risk of a storm tide event causing hundreds of deaths in London is regarded as tolerable even though it is 1 in 1000 per annum. It is not at all clear why, in principle, risks regarded as intolerable in one context should be seen as tolerable in another. The only conceivable justification is that the limit is chosen in light of what is reasonably practicable — it is reasonably practicable to reduce the risk around industrial installations to the levels proposed by the HSE, and it is not reasonably practicable to do so in the case of the Thames barrier. However, if this is the reasoning, it flies in the face of the whole tolerability framework which requires that the level of tolerability should be set independently of questions of reasonable practicability.

It is clear that the concepts of tolerable or acceptable risk in the context of multiple fatalities are even more questionable than they are for individual fatality risk. It makes sense to talk of approved risk in this context, for there is no normative claim involved in such language; however, to suggest that any level of risk is tolerable or intolerable based on the number of people likely to be killed, can only initiate pointless controversy.

Value of life

I return now to the second of Flüeler and Seiler's rules: risk should be reduced as far below the absolute limit or tolerability as is cost effective. The first step in applying this rule is to calculate the cost of a proposed risk reduction measure, estimate the number of lives which are likely to be saved by taking this measure, and compute a cost per life saved. In fact, Flüeler and Seiler go beyond this by noting that saving the life of a young person saves more "life-years" than saving the life of an older person. It is therefore possible to calculate the cost of the risk reduction measure per life-year saved, as well as per life saved.

To decide whether the proposed measure is cost effective requires a second step; namely, specifying how much it is worth spending to save a life, or a life-year. Flüeler and Seiler suggest that this depends on the degree to which the risk is voluntarily assumed. They suggest that the appropriate figure ranges from 1 and 20 million Swiss francs per life saved. Per life-year saved, the corresponding figures are 25 to 500,000 Swiss francs. These figures are based on empirical estimates of what it actually costs in certain arenas, but in the tolerability/acceptability framework, they become guidelines as to how much it is reasonable to spend on saving the lives of the risk-exposed. Inevitably this amounts to putting a value on human life, which raises obvious moral concerns.

There has been considerable discussion in the United Kingdom of how much is reasonable to spend on saving human life. In an apparent attempt to avoid the moral issue, the debate is phrased in terms of the "value of preventing a fatality" rather than the "value of saving a life"; but this is little more than a verbal switch and the moral concerns remain the same. The HSE suggests that the appropriate figure is about 1 million pounds, which is the same figure used by the United Kingdom Department of Transport for evaluating road accident prevention measures (HSE, 2001:36,65). This figure is derived from various studies of the public's "willingness to pay". However, in the case of the rail industry, the HSE accepts a figure of 3.2 million pounds (Uff and Cullen, 2001:44). It has been estimated that installing a Train Protection and Warning System (TPWS), to help avoid collisions, will cost 10 million pounds per fatality prevented, and the HSE has said that, notwithstanding the industry figure of 3.2 million, it considers this higher figure to be reasonable, "given the large numbers at risk and the widespread concern over safety on the railways" (Davies, 2003:20). The United Kingdom is in fact going ahead with a further system called Automatic Train Protection (ATP), at an additional cost per fatality prevented of 30 million pounds (Cullen, 2001:211).

The range of figures endorsed by the HSE and the decision to implement ATP, at 30 million pounds per fatality prevented, demonstrates the difficulty of making use of any such value as an independent benchmark against which to make cost-benefit decisions. The reality described above seems almost the reverse: expenditure decisions are made, the cost per fatality prevented is then calculated, and this cost per fatality is said to be justified by widespread public concern, or perhaps by political considerations, or the public's willingness to pay. In this case, therefore, the "value of a prevented fatality" is not an aid to decision making but an ex post facto, ad hoc rationalisation of the decision.

This is perhaps just as well. If a decision was made not to go ahead with a risk reduction project on the grounds that the cost per fatality prevented exceeded some agreed value, the moral question would again be raised as to whether this amounted to putting a value on human life.

The ethical problems involved in implicitly or explicitly putting a value on human life have been highlighted by various authors. Tweeddale, for example, notes (when considering industrial risks) that:

"A problem with using the value of life as the basis for setting the criterion [of what is reasonably practicable] is that, if it is decided that the monetary value of the lives saved is insufficient to justify the proposed expenditure on safeguards, the saving and the "costs" are directed to different groups: the saving being made by the organisation which avoids the need to install the safeguards, and the cost (in the form of the risks) being born by those exposed (2003:78)."

This comment is less applicable where costs of the safeguards are likely to be passed on directly to the risk-exposed, as they would be in the case of rail passengers, in the form of higher fares. But in the case of industrial safety, where the expenditure on safety will be in the first instance at the expense of owners and not workers, any decision that it is not cost effective to spend further resources very clearly benefits one group at the expense of another.[10]

There is one way in which the moral issue can be largely circumvented. Where there is a possibility of using funds on one or other of a number of possible risk reduction measures, it makes sense to calculate the cost per life saved for each measure and fund those interventions which give the greatest value for money in terms of lives saved. For example, it has been calculated in the United States that grooved pavements on highways would cost 29,000 dollars per life-year saved, while relocation of utility poles from 8 to 15 feet from the highway edge would cost 420,000 dollars per life-year saved (Tengs et al, 1995). Assuming highway authorities have a choice about how they spend their money, they can save many more lives for a given amount of money by grooving highways than by relocating light poles. The advantage of this analysis is that it in no way places an implicit value on life, and it involves no judgment about how much money should be spent. It is simply a guide to how to maximise the life-saving potential of available funds.

The preceding example cannot be generalised easily. In the debate about installing ATP in the United Kingdom, the point was often made that it would be far more cost effective to spend the money on preventing road fatalities. One estimate was that the cost to prevent a road fatality was about 0.1 million pounds as against the 30 million pounds for the ATP system (Cullen, 2001:211). In other words, if all the money earmarked for spending on ATP were spent instead on preventing road deaths, many more lives would be saved. The problem is, however, that the funds are not readily transferable. The funding for ATP will presumably come from the various rail organisations, to be recouped from rail passengers, while the resources needed to prevent road fatalities presumably comes from a number of government and non-government sources. In short, a decision not to spend money on ATP does not mean that the money will be spent instead on

---

10 The problems involved in putting a value on life are well discussed in Dorman, 1996: Ch 6. See also Adams, 1995: Ch 6.

reducing road fatalities. In general, wherever funds are non-transferable in this way, cost-benefit comparisons become largely irrelevant.

To summarise this section, the "value of life saved" approach is intended as a spending guide for those seeking to reduce risks as far as reasonably practicable. However, it turns out to be little more than a codification of what is in fact being spent to save life and as such loses much of its value as a decision-making criterion. It may perhaps help to standardise spending in a given industry or arena, but it is of little value in determining what that standard should be. Moreover, as the decisions about TPWS and ATP reveal, there are circumstances where it is no guide at all, until after the spending decisions have been made.

The idea of accidents as caused

Quantitative risk assessment is based on an assumption that accidents are fundamentally chance or random events and so can never be totally prevented, no matter what measures we take.

The alternative view is that accidents are caused and that the role of management is to identify and counter those causes. Time and again analyses of accidents occurring in an organisational context show that they occur because of the failure of some preventive measure or series of preventive measures that should have been in place. As Tweeddale notes, these are "driven failures, not random failures" (2003:202). It may be, for example, that systematic hazard identification procedures have not been carried out, auditing has been shallow, permit to work systems have not been implemented as required, preventive maintenance has not been done, procedures have been violated, and so on. Such measures are designed to prevent accidents and accidents can only occur if one or more of these measures fails. It is for this reason that the claim is often made that all accidents are preventable. All too often we hear that this was an accident "waiting to happen", meaning that those concerned knew beforehand that the hazards had not been properly controlled. When courts find, as they so often do, that it would have been reasonably practicable to prevent a particular accident, it is the failure or inadequacy of these preventive measures to which they refer. It is noteworthy that, in making such decisions, courts do not concern themselves with whether or not the overall level of risk to employees or other stakeholders has been driven down below the threshold of acceptable risk (Hopkins, 2002). The question is whether the risk in the current case was as low as reasonably practicable, and if it was not, the company will be found liable.[11] On this view, then, no specific death can be regarded as acceptable simply because the death rate or risk of death is acceptably low.

The style of accident analysis referred to above implicitly adopts a particular meaning of cause — necessary condition. Had any one of the failures identified in the analysis not occurred, the accident would not have happened. Each such failure was thus a precondition for the accident. This is not to say that such failures make an accident inevitable. An organisation may survive without an accident for a considerable time, despite the presence of a series of organisational failures or inadequacies, until some particular pattern of events triggers the accident. For this reason, these failures have sometimes been described as *latent* causes or conditions (Reason, 1997). In other words, identifying organisational failings does not enable us to predict that a particular accident will occur; it enables us simply to conclude that the risk of accident is unnecessarily high. Necessary conditions therefore amount to causes only in a relatively weak sense.

It can be argued, however, that the ultimate purpose of causal analysis is to be able to predict events, and this requires that we identify a set of conditions which together make the accident inevitable (Fischer, nd). Such a set of conditions would include all the background failures and all the immediate circumstances. The idea of cause as a set of sufficient conditions is clearly a much stronger notion of cause. However, identifying causes in this sense is far more difficult, indeed impossible in most situations. To predict in detail when and where a specific accident will take place would require far more information than is normally available.

This is not to say that predicting the future is impossible. Using powerful computers and masses of data, weather forecasters are becoming increasingly capable of predicting weather at least 24 hours in advance. In 1998, they predicted that an uncommonly intense storm would develop in a very specific location off the south east coast of Australia, just at the time the Sydney-Hobart yacht race was expected to pass through the area. Their prediction was not effectively relayed to race participants, but it proved to be accurate, and six yachtsmen died in the storm.[12] Of course, the weather forecasters were not in a position to predict that these particular people would die. However, if we had known something about the buoyancy characteristics of the boats, and

---

11   Rasmussen notes that many of the failures which give rise to accidents occur because of economic pressures and that therefore it is not appropriate to view accidents as chance events. Analyses of accidents, he says, "demonstrate that they have not been caused by a coincidence of independent failures and human errors, but by the systematic migration of organisational behaviour toward accident under the influence of pressure toward cost-effectiveness in an aggressive, competitive environment" (1997:189).

12   Chaos theory suggests that if we knew enough about the weather we might be able to show how a butterfly flapping its wings could initiate a chain of events leading to a storm on the other side of the world. The phenomenon is known as sensitive dependence on initial conditions (Gleick, 1998:23).

their predicted locations, it might well have been possible to predict which particular boats would get into trouble. In short, the more information that is available, the more specific the predictions can become.

The notion of cause in the strong sense seems ultimately incompatible with the idea of chance or randomness. If events are entirely predictable, then there is no room for random occurrences.[13] The notion of cause in the weaker sense is not, however, incompatible with chance, in principle. The absence of preventive measures does not make accidents inevitable, it merely makes them more likely, and it is arguable that whether or not they actually occur is still a matter of chance.

Nevertheless, in practice the whole framework of risk acceptability is jeopardised once we begin to identify necessary conditions which have allowed accidents to occur. Consider the following. In the United Kingdom, the annual risk of death from the use of gas in the home (by fire, explosion or carbon monoxide poisoning) is less than 1 in 1 million — 1 in 1.5 million, to be precise (HSE, 2001:44). Recall that the HSE regards a risk of 1 in 1 million as acceptable. However, gas deaths are viewed quite differently. As the HSE puts it, "gas incidents continue to give rise to societal concern, particularly where incidents occur because unscrupulous landlords seek to avoid the cost of simple safety checks on their gas heating systems and so put those who rent the accommodation (often young people) at greater risk". Such events are not seen as chance occurrences, the risk of which is so low as to be acceptable; rather they are seen as having a cause — the unscrupulous behaviour of landlords. As such they are entirely preventable and the HSE notes that it "has responded by firm enforcement action where appropriate, and by targeted publicity emphasising the importance of annual gas checks".

Here, then, is a case in which the HSE does not adopt a do-nothing approach because of the very low level of the risk. Indeed, it is arguable that the very low level is precisely because of the activities of the regulator and that, in the absence of this activity, the number of gas-related deaths in the home would rise to barely tolerable or even intolerable levels.

It might be argued the level of risk where landlords do not carry out safety checks is much higher than 1 in 1 million and that it is this risk that justifies the more vigorous response. But the HSE has not tried to quantify this heightened risk in order to justify its actions. Rather it points to "societal concern" in these circumstances as its justification. It seems likely that this societal concern arises from the fact that these deaths are easily preventable, that landlords are obliged to take steps to prevent them, and that their failure to do so is therefore culpable.

---

13   Vatn suggests that randomness does not exist as such. Rather, the limitations on our knowledge make it quite impossible to predict most events, and we therefore invoke the concept of randomness to deal with this uncertainty (1998:3).

The chance of dying from the use of gas in the home in the United Kingdom is not so very different from the chance of being killed by lightning,[14] but the response is very different. As has already been noted, death by lightning strike is generally viewed as a random event and a matter of very bad luck. The difference is instructive. We know enough about the causes of home gas incidents to be able to prevent them; we don't know enough about the weather to be able to predict lightning strikes and so prevent the occasional death by lightning. In the former case we are inclined to adopt the cause/prevention paradigm, while in the latter we are inclined to adopt the paradigm of chance and acceptable risk.

Reducing risk by reducing exposure

One of the paradoxical consequences of the risk acceptability framework is that it can sometimes distract attention from the need to identify hazards and put in place controls. This comes about in the following way. QRA seeks to quantify the risk to the individual and to encourage employers/operators to drive these risks below some predetermined level of tolerability or acceptability. One way to do this is to reduce the risk that an accident will occur, but the risk to individuals can also be reduced simply by reducing their exposure to a possible accident event.

Such thinking drives decisions about the siting of housing estates adjacent to dangerous installations. Given that the risk of a major accident at such an installation is not zero, the risk to residents can be kept below whatever limit of acceptability is chosen by maintaining sufficient separation between any houses and the plant. It is hard to fault such decision making, but one consequence should be noted. Given the higher level of risk to which employees may be subject, the plant may not be required to carry out risk reduction activities to the same extent as would have been required had it been located immediately adjacent to a housing estate.

Consider now the case of a petroleum company operating offshore which requires some of its workers to pay frequent visits to unmanned platforms. In order to keep the risk to which each of these people is exposed within the limits of acceptability, the company restricts the number of flights which each such employee makes. The helicopter operator keeps a tally and when the limit is approached the worker will be taken off this job and another will take his place. In this way the company honours its commitment to individual workers not to expose them to more than the acceptable level of risk.

---

14   In the United Kingdom, 1 in 19 million (HSE, 2001:70); in Australia, 1 in 8 million (Higson, 1989:33).

Notice that this strategy does nothing to limit the risk that *someone* will be killed; it merely spreads the risk over a larger group of employees. Moreover, from a company point of view, the risk that someone (anyone) will be killed is the relevant risk. A fatality will cause unpredictable disruptions, the possibility of enforcement action and immeasurable psychological damage to all who are close to the person or persons killed. The company has an interest in driving the risk of any fatality as low as possible and its focus on individual fatality risk inevitably distracts it from this goal.

Consider, finally, the petroleum company which reduced the number of helicopter flights to compensate for the increased risk from the gas compressor. This was a strategy which concentrated exclusively on reducing exposure. It accepted the risks inherent in compressors and helicopter flights as given, and did nothing to reduce the inherent dangers of either. It was a strategy that ignored or perhaps simply accepted the fact that the platform would henceforth be at greater risk of fire as a result of the new compressor.

Calculating risks

So far this discussion has been about the acceptability of risk; nothing has been said about exactly how organisations go about calculating the risks to which their stakeholders are exposed. This is an area which raises additional concerns about the adequacy of the whole acceptable risk framework.

In some contexts, calculating the risk is relatively straightforward. For railway workers, for example, one possibility is to divide the number of fatalities per year by the number of railway employees. Some rail employees, such as track-side workers, are much more exposed than others, so to obtain a more meaningful picture it is preferable to calculate a rate for this group separately. If we make the assumption that such workers are all equally exposed to risk over the course of a year, their fatality rate can be taken as an indication of risk.[15]

Suppose, however, one is wanting to quantify the risk of a major fire at some hazardous installation, such as a proposed new offshore petroleum production platform. An obvious starting point is to look for historical data on the number of major fires at hazardous installations so as to be able to calculate a rate. But what is the population of installations for which the rate is to be calculated? It could be argued that the risks in chemical processing plants are systematically different from those in petroleum production installations and the former should therefore be excluded from the calculation. Similarly, onshore oil and gas processing plants are systematically different from offshore facilities and need to be excluded. Furthermore, existing offshore platforms were built to less stringent standards and their experience

---

15 The assumption is, of course, questionable.

is therefore not relevant. In this way we rapidly arrive at the conclusion that the historical data on fires in hazardous installations is of no value in assessing the risk at our proposed new platform. This is a case where the rate, no matter how defined, provides no indication of the risk.

In these circumstances, QRA adopts a different approach. It seeks to identify every possible way in which a major fire might develop and assess the probability of each such scenario. For example, a valve might fail on a compressor releasing a large amount of gas, a hole might develop in a high-pressure gas line as a result of corrosion, and so on. Industry data exists on the probability of such occurrences and this can then be used as a starting point. Knowledge of the particular installation can be used to identify potential ignition points and hence the likelihood of ignition. Adding together all these risks yields the overall risk of fire. The probability that an individual will be in the area can also be estimated and in this way the risk to an individual can be calculated. Production workers are more likely to be in the area than, for example, catering staff, and so their risk will be greater.

Other kinds of risks can then be computed; for example, the risk of an aircraft crash en route to and from the platform, and a total risk for individuals in various categories can be estimated. These are then expressed as the individual risk per annum or the fatality rate per annum expected for workers with a specified pattern of risk exposure; that is, in a specified category.

Making these calculations is a formidable task involving a substantial commitment of resources but the end result is a figure for each category of workers which can then be compared with the risk acceptance criterion, say 1 in 1000, to assess whether the risk to which an individual is exposed is within the limits of tolerability.

As can be imagined, a host of assumptions are made in the process of carrying out these calculations. Here is an example. At one installation, workers fly in and out in fixed wing aircraft. The aircraft are chartered. Chartered aircraft have a higher accident rate than regular passenger aircraft. However, the risk analysts decided not to use the accident rate for chartered aircraft because the charterer in this case is a large airline that operates the charter flight much like a regular passenger service. The decision was no doubt justified in this case, but it provides an example of the discretion available to analysts in deciding what kind of industry data to incorporate into their models. It can be assumed that this discretion will often be exercised in such a way as to reduce the calculated risk. Indeed, one hears stories about risk analysts experimenting with different assumptions in an effort to bring the results in under the limits of tolerability (see also Tweeddale, 2003:206).

Apart from this, the generic data may be of very doubtful relevance to the particular case. An Australian QRA firm notes, for example, that the use of generic pipeline failure rates:

"... does not take into consideration improvement in manufacturing and monitoring standards, or the possibility that local systems are superior to world standards. Failure rates also do not take into account land use. For example, third party pipeline damage is far more likely in a rural area than in a major city street (R2A, 2002:11.13)."

There is another, probably more fundamental, problem associated with this type of QRA — it fails to acknowledge the crucial role of human factors. Admittedly, there have been some attempts to take human error into account. For example, it is estimated that the probability of dialling ten consecutive digits wrongly is 6 in 100, while the probability of failing to notice that a valve is in the wrong position is one in two.[16]

However, accident research shows that it is not just errors of this type which trigger accidents, but phenomena which defy quantification, such as poor procedures, violations of procedures, and plain ignorance. For example, the Piper Alpha disaster got underway because of a failure in the permit to work system. The inadequacy in the permit system was longstanding but had not been picked up in auditing. This is essentially a management failure which would be impossible to incorporate into a quantitative risk assessment.

Take another example. To estimate the risk of valve failure from industry data is to ignore the fact that the likelihood of valve failure in any particular situation may be almost wholly determined by the behaviour of employees and their managers on the spot. If routine maintenance work is not being done as a result of financial cutbacks, the risk of valve failure will be much higher. Even more dramatically, if employees have disabled valves for some reason, these valves will certainly fail to function as designed when the need arises. This is precisely what happened at the Kaiser alumina plant in Louisiana in 1999 when an explosion injured 29 people. Industry data on valve failure provide no indication of the risks involved in these circumstances.

Putting all this another way, the quality of management will have a major effect on risk. Poor management could conceivably increase the risks ten or even a hundred fold. In other words, although a quantitative risk assessment might assess the risks to be tolerable, inadequate management could drive the true risks well above the limit of tolerability.[17] Conversely, good management may reduce risks to well below any quantitatively assessed level.

QRA has been subjected to some very harsh criticism along these lines by some of its own practitioners. For example, Robert Bea, after three decades of carrying out quantitative risk assessments, has come to the view that QRAs

---

16   R2A, 2002:6.9. Tweeddale (2003:371,375) demonstrates just how problematic these probabilities are.

17   Tweeddale makes a similar point (2002:201,214). He argues that the effects of poor management cannot be included in a QRA and any attempt to do so is pure guesswork. He concludes bluntly that poor management simply invalidates a QRA.

are being widely misused. Engineers working for organisations are inevitably biased in the direction of underestimating the risk, he says. Moreover, their primary purpose is to "produce elegant analytic models", and they "start believing that the numbers represent reality". He concludes that "the marked limitations of analytical models and quantitative methods must be recognized or major damage can be done to the cause of system safety" (1996:1; 1999:5).

Petroleum industry engineer Graham Dalzell is similarly critical. He argues that, because of QRA's emphasis on finding appropriate data to be used in risk calculations, it tends in practice to distract attention from the hunt for possible causes of major accidents in petrochemical facilities. Efforts should be focused, he says, not on locating appropriate "historical data but on a rigorous examination of the plant, the causes of failure and the effectiveness of prevention systems. ... the first step in risk reduction is either to eliminate the cause or to improve the prevention system" (nd:6).

The preceding analysis has been largely critical of QRA because of the ways in which it is often used. It is not my intention, however, to dismiss QRA entirely. Its advocates argue quite persuasively that it can be an aid to decision making provided its limitations are kept in mind. In his discussion of the strengths and weaknesses of QRA, Tweeddale notes that:

> "... the value of the assessments lies not in the bottom line [of computed risk], which is usually of too dubious precision or applicability to be relied on, but in the insights gained in undertaking the analysis, and the relative magnitudes of the components of the assessed risk (2003:206)."

Conclusion

This analysis has uncovered two competing conceptions of how accidents occur, one is that they are caused, and the other is that they occur by chance. QRA and its associated concepts of acceptable or tolerable risk are based on the latter conception. Discussion here has focused on the limitations of QRA in providing guidance on just how far organisations should go in seeking to improve safety. As we have seen, there are various ethical and other difficulties in determining the limits of tolerability, and there are enormous if not insuperable difficulties in quantifying risk in any particular context in order to be able to compare it against benchmark figures. The most significant risk is poor management and this is inherently unquantifiable. QRA is largely inappropriate, therefore, as a means of deciding whether risk has been driven to a sufficiently low level. In particular, it should never be allowed to override sound professional judgments about necessary risk reduction measures. It can, however, have more modest uses, such as helping to determine priorities.

The alternative paradigm, that accidents are caused, is fundamental to accident prevention. Only by knowing their causes can accidents be prevented. Moreover, causation is the starting point in any legal inquiry. A finding of legal liability is a finding that an accident was caused by the duty-holder, and that it could and should have been prevented. This is the very antithesis of randomness. Given that organisational accidents in which people are killed or injured frequently give rise to findings of either criminal or civil liability, it is clear that the courts routinely reject the notion of accidents as chance events.[18]

There are tensions, therefore, between the tolerability framework and the way cases are decided in courts. These tensions are partly a result of the difference in how accidents are understood — chance events versus caused events. But they arise, also, from different ways of deciding how low risk needs to be driven. At law, employers must drive risks down as far as is reasonably practicable, and there is no level of risk which, a priori, can be said to be acceptable.[19] Moreover, the law has a well-developed set of principles for determining whether risks are as low as reasonably practicable, and despite the indeterminacy of these principles, it is by no means clear that QRA and the tolerability/acceptability framework offers a better way of deciding how low is low enough. In short, risk-aware organisations need to be very wary of quantitative risk assessment.

---

18   But not always. Courts will sometimes take the view that an accident was a chance event which it was not reasonably practicable for an employer to prevent. See *Marshall v Gotham* [1954] AC 360.

19   Viner (2002:12) makes a similar point.

Chapter 13
Risk society?

One of the enduring aims of social theory is to capture the essence of contemporary society in a single term. We live, it seems, in "post-modern", "post-industrial", "neo-liberal", "global" or "globalised" society, depending on which aspect of social reality the theorist wishes to make central to the analysis. One of the more intriguing of these terms is "risk society", popularised by German sociologist Ulrich Beck (1992). Risk has become a major theme of social theory and the value of the term "risk society" has been much debated by sociologists. Most readers of this book will be unaware of the debate but will no doubt be curious about the idea, just as sociologists have been. My purpose here is to review some of the debate and to ask the question: does Beck's concept of risk society live up to its promise as a way of understanding contemporary reality?

Beck's thesis

Beck starts by noting that industrial society is dominated by the logic of wealth production and distribution, by which he means that society is organised around the production of wealth and that political activity involves a struggle over the distribution of this wealth, with some political parties advocating more redistributive measures than others. Traditional industrial society, then, is a class society, in the sense that it is made up of economically defined classes, in conflict over the distribution of the economic rewards.

In contrast, risk society is dominated by the logic of risk production and distribution. And whereas in class society the distribution of wealth benefits some at the expense of others, in risk society the distribution of risk is universal, in that risks boomerang on their creators (1992:23). For example, those who use toxic pesticides and herbicides to boost food production end up ingesting those toxins along with the rest of us. According to Beck, such risks are democratic in that they affect all of us: "poverty is hierarchic, smog is democratic" (1992:36). The distinctive risks of our time, such as atmospheric pollution, are global in reach, he says (1992:21), and they threaten the "self-destruction of all life on Earth" (1992:21). Ultimately, no-one can escape.

One objection which might be raised at this point is that it is simply not true that we are equally exposed to environmental risks. Those who can afford to move away from smog and pollution do so. In other words, even some of these most democratic of risks are distributed to some extent by class.

A second objection is that modern society still very obviously involves a struggle over scarce resources and the logic of industrial society remains a dominant logic. In no sense can it be said that risk society has replaced class society. Beck concedes this point and he suggests that we do not yet live in risk society. Even in West Germany, where the process has gone the furthest, the transition from wealth-distributing to risk-distributing society has just begun (1992:20). Risk society is society of the future, not of the present, he says. Yet much of his analysis presumes that risk society is already here; that is indeed why the idea has such appeal. This is a serious ambiguity in his work.

What, then, does Beck mean by risk? In many contexts, risk refers to probability, and in some contexts the concept of risk involves multiplying the probability by some measure of severity of outcome (Pybus, 1996). But in Beck's work, risk has little to do with probability and is used interchangeably with danger or hazard. Moreover, whereas in many discourses the word risk is used in an emotionally neutral way, Beck's usage always carries with it the connotation of dread that is associated with the word danger (Douglas, 1992:45; Turner, 1995:225).

It is easy to interpret Beck as saying that we live in an era of unprecedented risk, that is, unprecedented danger. If this is indeed his claim, it is dubious. The risks of previous centuries were just as widespread as the risks of modern society. Plague, for example, was capable of wiping out vast numbers of people, and death in childbirth was a risk to which very many women succumbed. Beck acknowledges this point. "It is not clear [he says] whether it is the risks that have intensified or our view of them" (1992:55). Is Beck's thesis, then, simply about perceptions? Is it simply that we now live with a greater fear of danger than in the past?

According to the English social theorist, Allan Scott, this is indeed what Beck is saying: we live now in a society consumed with anxiety. Beck's risk society is really no more than "angst society". Scott argues that this is a specifically German point of view. He quotes one German politician as saying, "We Germans are the world's champions at anxiety" (2000:39).

However, if the essence of Beck's claim is merely that we live in an era of unprecedented *anxiety*, this, too, is dubious. Europe in the middle ages was obsessed with danger. "Fears of the real and imaginary abounded. ...Villagers and townspeople closed themselves in their dwellings at night, not daring to go out once darkness had fallen, because night was considered the domain of all danger: the kingdom of the Devil, of demons, of witches and werewolves and monstrous beasts" (Lupton, 1999:2). It is not at all obvious that modern society is now more fearful than societies of the past.

Beck's risks

To move beyond this impasse, let us consider in more detail the risks of which Beck speaks in his book, *Risk Society*. They fall, for the most part, into three categories. First, there are major accidents, such as nuclear reactor incidents resulting in the emission of large amounts of radiation, of which Chernobyl, 1986, is the outstanding example (Marples, 1988). Other examples of accidents are the uncontrolled release of chemicals at Bhopal in 1984, which resulted in thousands of deaths, and the Exxon Valdez oil spill in Alaskan waters in 1989. The second category of risk about which Beck speaks is industrial pollution, particularly of the atmosphere. One consequence of this is the acid rain which has killed significant areas of forest in the northern hemisphere. The third category is the presence of toxic chemicals in our food, resulting in many cases from the use of fertilisers and pesticides. These three categories of risk are the things about which Beck is most concerned. These things threaten to make the Earth uninhabitable (1992:38), and constitute a scorched earth policy (1992:38); they are "dangers running wild" (1992:46).

Various other risks are mentioned in passing but do not receive anything like the attention of the above three categories. The risks of unemployment, stress and *occupational* exposure to toxic chemicals are once mentioned (1992:35) in order to make the point that some risks may be distributed by class, but these risks make no further appearance since they are clearly not the kinds of risk which threaten the "self-destruction of all life on Earth".

Other risks of our age which are either dismissed or not mentioned at all are the risk of death from traffic accidents, suicide, land mines, famine and mass shootings by deranged individuals. These are clearly significant hazards but are not part of Beck's concern.

One other risk which is notably absent from Beck's treatment is AIDS. The English edition of his book was published with a specially written introduction and preface in 1992, long after the threat of AIDS had been well established. Yet no mention is made of this most menacing of dangers. One merciful aspect of the AIDS virus is that it is not readily transmissible. Surely one of the greatest dangers we face — one which *does* have the capacity to destroy all *human* life on Earth — is the prospect that the netherworld of rapidly mutating viruses will sooner or later throw up an organism as infectious as influenza and as long lasting and deadly as AIDS. This would seem to be as plausible a threat to our species as any of those which Beck discusses. The recent epidemic of SARS (Severe Acute Respiratory Syndrome) serves to highlight this possibility.

Finally, global terrorism has become one of the risks of great concern in the 21st century. Understandably, this is not a risk that figures in Beck's analysis.

Explaining Beck's selection of risks

It is clear that Beck has been rather selective in the risks he chooses to emphasise. How can his choice be explained? Obviously they are matters of great public concern in Germany which is, after all, the cradle of Green politics. However, are there any more fundamental reasons?

Beck characterises the new dangers as global and largely irreversible. But they are not all global; indeed, toxic accidents such as Bhopal have highly localised effects. Nor are they necessarily irreversible, as the clean up of smog in some of the cities of the advanced world demonstrates.

Could it be that the risks Beck emphasises are in some sense the most serious? Not in any obvious sense. In terms of sheer numbers killed, motor accidents and famine would have to rank higher.

Are they perhaps the distinctive risks of modern times? It is true that technological/industrial accidents involving hundreds or even thousands of deaths, and threatening the health of thousands more, are a distinctive feature of our times. But so, too, are motor vehicle accidents.

Again, industrial pollution is a fairly contemporary risk, dating back only a century or two. But the problem of pollution from *industrial* effluent has strong parallels with the problem of pollution caused by *human* effluent, which has a far longer history. Wherever people lived in large concentrations they were subject to deadly diseases generated by unsanitary conditions. Such risks, as others have pointed out (Turner, 1995:224), were just as severe and just as democratic — in that they affected rich and poor alike — as the risks to which Beck has drawn attention. While industrial pollution may be a distinctive feature of our times, pollution per se is not.

So how are we to understand Beck's selection of risks and his hyperbole about them? I want to argue in what follows that the key characteristic of these risks is that they involve some attribution of responsibility or even blame. Beck himself discusses processes of blame attribution which operate in connection with some of the risks he identifies. Here are his words:

> "Businesses that had long been pampered in a cosy capitalist consensus ... suddenly find themselves on the witness bench, or more precisely, locked in the pillory, and confronted with the kind of questions that were previously used to prosecute poisoners caught red-handed ... (1992:76)."

He goes on:

> "Economic and technological details are investigated in the light of a *new* ecological morality. Anyone on a crusade against pollutants must scrutinise the industrial operations from the eco-moral point of view (1992:77, his emphasis)."

Elsewhere he talks of the politics of identifying the "guilty parties" who create the risks (1992:31).

Blame and responsibility are thus important features of Beck's analysis. However, they are not presented as *defining* features. Beck purports to identify the risks of concern in terms of their unprecedented and global effects and then goes on to talk about the processes of blame attribution which operate in relation to these risks. I want to turn this on its head. I have shown earlier that Beck's risks cannot be distinguished from other risks in terms of their effects. What distinguishes them, I believe, is precisely the fact that they are seen to be blameworthy.

The point is best made by considering some of the risks about which Beck is silent. Take AIDS. No particular group and no organisation is responsible for its spread and it is not easy to attribute blame for this disaster. If anyone is blamed, it is the victims themselves. In this respect, AIDS has some of the characteristics of a natural disaster. If anyone is blamed for the devastation caused by flooding it is the victims themselves who have chosen to build in flood-prone areas.

Again, it is difficult to identify credible perpetrators who can be held responsible for the road toll. Attempts to assign blame usually focus on drivers who are frequently also the victims. In the case of the pollution caused by human effluent in previous centuries, it is particularly difficult to assign blame in any credible way. Similar points can be made about many of the other undoubtedly serious hazards which Beck has not made central to his analysis.

What seems to emerge from this discussion is that it is the very fact that we can credibly identify guilty parties and thus assign blame that distinguishes the risks about which Beck is concerned from other equally serious dangers about which he is not. The defining characteristic of the risks about which Beck is concerned is not that they are technological in origin, nor that they are global in reach, but that they are seen by relevant audiences as blameworthy. Perhaps, then, Beck's risk society is really "blame society".

Douglas on blame

Interpreted in this way, Beck's analysis is quite similar to that of social theorist Mary Douglas, who argues that what is characteristic of modern society is a tendency to allocate blame for every misfortune. She provides an interesting historical analysis of this tendency to blame.

In non-modern cultures, misfortunes of all kinds could be laid at someone's feet (Douglas, 1992:5). If a woman died it may be that *she* was to blame — she had offended the ancestors, broken a taboo, etc. Or possibly an adversary or enemy had contrived her death by witchcraft. One way or another, her death was blamed on someone. In such societies, Douglas argues, there is no such thing as a natural death. Furthermore, if crops failed it was because someone had angered the gods. Indeed the "the stronger the solidarity of a community, the more readily will natural disasters be coded as signs of reprehensible behaviour" (1992:6).

According to Douglas, by the mid 20th century, the march of science had enabled us to provide rational explanations for almost every kind of misfortune. No longer did danger or misfortune provide an opportunity to assign blame. The link between danger and morality had been broken: "morals were to be enforced by moral persuasion and danger was known by technology" (1992:9). Death was no longer the result of the nefarious activities of others; instead, doctors' certificates noted that death was from "natural" causes. Quoting the anthropologist Levy-Bruhl, Douglas and her co-author Wildavsky suggest that "the distinctive achievement [of the recent past] was to invent the idea of natural death and actually believe in it" (1982:31).

However, this idea of natural death (and more generally, misfortune) for which no-one was to blame turned out to be relatively short lived. In present-day society, death has come to be seen as caused by something for which someone else is responsible. As Douglas says, "we are ... almost ready to treat every death as chargeable to someone's account, every accident as caused by someone's criminal negligence, every sickness a threatened prosecution. Whose fault? is the first question" (1992:15-16). In this respect we have reverted to "primitive cultures whose views on death and misfortune we recently congratulated ourselves on having transcended" (Douglas and Wildavsky, 1982:33).

Douglas and Wildavsky offer various explanations for this increasing tendency to blame. One of the more plausible explanations concerns the distinction between voluntary and involuntary risks. There is a widespread feeling that if we *choose* to accept risks, that is our business and no-one else is to blame. Thus if we choose to participate in sports such as rock climbing or hang-gliding and are killed or injured, there is little tendency for blame to be laid at the feet of others. On the other hand, we feel angry if we are involuntarily exposed to risks by others, particularly if we are unaware that this has happened. Thus, if without knowing it we are exposed to toxic chemicals which threaten our lives, we are very prone to blame the perpetrators. The distinction between voluntary and involuntary risks is not a hard and fast one, and risks which from some perspectives appear voluntary are often matters over which we have no real choice. For instance, if someone accepts a dangerous job rather than remain unemployed, is this risk voluntarily borne? Despite such problems, there is a widespread perception that risks can be divided in this way and that is all that matters for the purposes of the argument.

Furthermore, because of the scale of technology and bureaucracy we are increasingly exposed to involuntary risks. Hence the increasing tendency to blame. As Douglas and Wildavsky put it:

> "If people are being increasingly deprived of control over their lives, if the march of big bureaucracy incorporates yearly larger proportions of the population in its ranks, people feel helpless — then their sense of outrage at involuntary risks will naturally grow more intense (1982:17)."

Environmental dangers are largely of this involuntary kind. Hence the passion with which the environmental movement blames polluters.

Another factor which Douglas and Wildavsky identify as contributing to the rise of blame is scientific knowledge itself. Whereas science in the mid 20th century presented misfortune as part of the natural order of things, the search for causes and risk factors has now facilitated the identification of guilty parties. Careful epidemiological studies have enabled us to demonstrate excess mortality caused by various environmental contaminants and food additives as well as by lifestyle factors such as smoking, lack of exercise and obesity. While the latter tend to implicate the victim in his or her own death, the former lay the blame for death squarely at the feet of particular industries or even enterprises. Quoting Douglas and Wildavsky again, "in the amazingly short space of fifteen or twenty years, confidence about the physical world has turned into doubt. Once a source of safety, science and technology have become a source of risk" (1982:11). What they mean by this is that science is now identifying the culprits who are causing our deaths; it is in this sense that death is no longer a natural event.

The analysis provided by Douglas and Wildavsky is questionable at many points and their purportedly historical account is so general and schematic as to be almost "ahistorical". But the virtue of their discussion is that it highlights blame as one of the central features of modern society and provides some support for the interpretation I have offered of Beck.

Outrage and betrayal

In one of the quotations above, Douglas and Wildavsky speak of the growth of a sense of outrage. The idea is worth elaborating for in some ways it goes beyond blame. According to one observer, major accidents can generate veritable "explosions of outrage" (Horlick-Jones, 1995:312). When trains crash or petrochemical plants explode killing large numbers of people, there is widespread fury and a demand for retribution which do not seem explicable simply in terms of the involuntary nature of risks to which the victims were subjected.

To understand this fury, we need to note that it is never suggested to the public that these technologies are inherently risky. On the contrary, modern technology promises control over the hazards in question and we accept these promises and believe the assurances of operators that their operations are safe. When it turns out that they are not, we feel a sense of betrayal. It is not so much that the risks have been imposed on us that generates a sense of rage and betrayal, but the fact that the promised control over those risks has failed. Furthermore, public rage is fuelled by the fact that investigations invariably demonstrate that the organisations in which we had put our faith behaved with a surprising degree of negligence. As an inquiry judge put it on one occasion: "from top to bottom the body corporate was infected with the disease of sloppiness" (Wells, 1993:47).

The development of legislation which enables organisations to be prosecuted for manslaughter is a manifestation of this outrage. The fact that this is happening in many jurisdictions is perhaps the clearest indicator of the very significant social change which has occurred in this respect.

Some commentators have interpreted this anger as an indicator that we live in an increasingly risk-averse society. But this misses the point. The fact is we live in a society in which it is possible to keep technological risks thoroughly under control, and where failures of control are therefore seen as culpable. Every death in these circumstances turns out to have been needless, and it is this, rather than any presumed aversion to risk, that generates public anger.

Contemporary society is not simply blame society. The feelings at times are stronger than that. When major accidents occur there is outrage and a sense of betrayal, stemming from the fact that the implicit promises that such accidents will not happen have been broken. This is something which the analysis by Douglas and Wildavsky fails to comprehend.

Conclusion

Where does this leave Beck's concept of risk society? It is hard to argue that risks have increased and it is equally difficult to suggest that our fear of risk has grown. What *is* true is that our ability to control risks of many kinds has increased and there is a reasonable expectation that hazards will be kept under control.

Contemporary society, then, is not one in which "dangers run wild", as Beck suggests. On the contrary, it is one in which they can be controlled. It is the possibility of control, indeed the promise of control, which makes the loss of control so intolerable and it is this that generates the blame, the explosions of outrage, which seem to be one of the features of our time. To return to an earlier theme, this is really the external, societal source of the pressure on political and organisational leaders to create cultures of safety.

Appendix

Safeworking Unit 245

**Passing an automatic signal at stop –
Automatic and Track Control (Bi-directional)**

procedures for signallers, handsignallers, drivers

[a]

■ Automatic signals at stop must only be passed:

either when the signal has failed and the driver has the verbal authority of the signaller or the authority of a green **caution** handsignal displayed by a handsignaller positioned at the signal and working under the instructions of the signaller

or when the driver is instructed by the signaller to assist a disabled train

or if the signal is fitted with a train stop and the train is fitted with a trip valve,	**or if** the signal is **not** fitted with a train stop **or if** the train is **not** fitted with a trip valve,
when the driver can see that the line ahead is unoccupied	when the signaller cannot be contacted by telephone and the driver has waited one minute and can see that the line ahead is unoccupied.

Passing an automatic signal at stop – Automatic and Track Control

To authorise a train to pass an automatic signal at stop   [b]

■ When a signaller becomes aware that an automatic signal has failed and it is considered necessary for train working purposes to position a handsignaller at the signal, every effort must be made by the signaller and the controlling station master to provide a handsignaller as soon as possible.

signaller at B **When** contacted on the signal telephone by the driver of a train at an automatic signal at stop or by a handsignaller positioned at an automatic signal:

1 Ask for the identification number of the signal.

2 Establish whether the line ahead is occupied or whether the signal has failed:

by checking the track indicator diagram, where provided, to establish whether a train is occupying the line between the signal where the train is standing and the next signal

and by checking the train register book or other recording system to establish if a train is still in the section

and by contacting the signaller at A to confirm the number of the last train which departed from A ahead of the train standing at the signal

If the line ahead is occupied:

3 Inform the driver or handsignaller of the reason for the delay.

4 Give the driver, or instruct the handsignaller to give the driver, one of the following instructions:

either to wait at the signal until the signal displays a proceed indication

or to wait at the signal for further instructions

or to pass the signal at stop, proceed with extreme caution and assist the disabled train.

If the signal has failed:

3 When you are satisfied that:

the section in advance is unoccupied

and that sufficient time has elapsed to permit the previous train to have passed completely beyond the signal ahead of the failed signal

and that it is safe for the train to proceed

advise the driver or handsignaller that the signal has failed.

| Safeworking systems on track-circuited double lines | SWU **245** |

4 **Either** authorise the driver to pass the signal at stop **or** authorise the handsignaller to display a green **caution** handsignal as the authority for the driver to pass the signal at stop.

5 Advise the drivers of all following trains, if possible before they enter the section, of the identification number of the failed signal(s).

handsignaller 1 Display a red handsignal to any approaching train until you are instructed otherwise by the signaller.

2 When a train arrives at the signal, advise the driver why the signal is at stop.

3 When authorised by the signaller, display a green **caution** handsignal to the driver as authority for the driver to proceed.

To pass an automatic signal at stop [c]

■ A signal at stop may have failed to clear as a result of a train on the line ahead, a broken rail or some other factor(s) affecting the track circuit and signal(s). For this reason, a driver must exercise extreme caution when passing a signal at stop.

■ When a train passes an automatic signal at stop, the driver must proceed with extreme caution to the first signal ahead of the signal at stop, prepared to stop short of any obstruction, and obey the indication of that signal. If it is displaying a proceed indication, the driver must proceed with extreme caution to the second signal agead of the signal at stop and obey the indication of that signal.

If there is a handsignaller positioned at the signal:

driver 1 Stop at the signal.

2 If necessary, find out from the handsignaller why the signal is at stop.

3 When the handsignaller display a green **caution** handsignal, pass the signal at stop.

Passing an automatic signal at stop – Automatic and Track Control

If there is no handsignaller positioned at the signal *and* the signal is fitted with a train stop *and* the train is fitted with a trip valve:

driver 1 Stop at the signal.

2 **either**

If you can see that the line ahead is unoccupied, trip past the signal at stop.

■ Drivers of electric trains must inform the guard, by bell code, that the train will trip past the signal.

or

If you can see a train occupying the line between the signal at which your train is standing and the next signal ahead, contact the signaller by signal telephone:

If contact can be made with the signaller:	If contact **cannot** be made with the signaller:
give the signaller the identification number of the signal at which your train is standing	**either** wait until the signal displays a proceed indication
then establish the cause of the delay	**or** when you can see that the train ahead has proceeded, wait until sufficient time has elapsed for it to have passed completely beyond the signal ahead of the signal at which you are standing and, if the signal fails to clear, pass the signal at stop.
then act as instructed by the signaller	

If there is *no* handsignaller positioned at the signal *and either* the signal does not have a train stop *or* the train is not fitted with a trip valve:

driver 1 Stop at the signal.

2 Contact the signaller by telephone.

3 **If** contact can be made with the signaller:	3 **If** contact **cannot** be made with the signaller:
give the signaller the identification number of the signal at which your train is standing	wait one minute and then, provided you can see that the line ahead is unoccupied, pass the signal at stop.
then establish the cause of the delay	
then act as instructed by the signaller.	

References

Adams J (1995), *Risk*, University College of London Press, London.

Appleton B (2001), "Piper Alpha" in T Kletz, *Learning from Accidents*, 3rd ed, Gulf, Oxford, pp 196-206.

ATSB (Australian Transport Safety Bureau) (2000), *Collision between Freight Train 9784 and Ballast Train 9795, Ararat, Victoria, 26 November 1999*, ATSB, Canberra.

Bea R (1996), "Quantitative risk analyses — the safety of offshore platforms", paper presented at the 28th Annual Offshore Technology Conference, Houston.

Bea R (1999), "Human and organisational factors in quality and reliability of engineering systems", proceedings of Seminar on Managing Safety in Hazardous Processes, Melbourne.

Beck U (1992), *Risk Society*, Sage, London.

BMA (British Medical Association) (1990), *BMA Guide to Living with Risk*, Penguin, Harmondsworth.

Bendix R (1966), *Max Weber: An Intellectual Portrait*, Methuan, London.

Berger Y (1999), "Why hasn't it changed on the shopfloor?", in C Mayhew and C Peterson (eds), *Occupational Health and Safety in Australia*, Allen & Unwin, Sydney.

Brooks A (1993), *Occupational Health and Safety Law in Australia*, CCH, Sydney.

Clarke L (1994), "Review of Beck's Risk Society", *Social Forces*, vol 73, pp 328-329.

Clarkson J, A Hopkins and K Taylor (2001), *The Report of the F111 Deseal/Reseal Board of Inquiry*, The Royal Australian Air Force, Canberra, available online at www.defence.gov.au/raaf/organisation/info_on/units/f111/volume1.htm.

Cullen L (1990), *The Public Inquiry into the Piper Alpha Disaster*, HMSO, London.

Cullen L (2001), *The Ladbroke Grove Rail Inquiry, Part 2*, HMSO, Norwich.

Dalzell G (nd), "From ignorance to enlightenment: a study of implementing change", unpublished paper.

Davies P (2003), "Regulation: death by a thousand cuts", *The Chemical Engineer*, February, p 20.

Dawson D and B Brooks (1999), *Report of the Longford Royal Commission: The Esso Gas Plant Accident*, Government Printer of the State of Victoria, Melbourne.

Dorman P (1996), *Markets and Mortality: Economics, Dangerous Work and the Value of Human Life*, Cambridge University Press, Cambridge.

Douglas M and A Wildavsky (1982), *Risk and Culture: An Essay on the Selection of Technical and Environmental Dangers*, University of California Press, Berkeley.

Douglas M (1992), *Risk and Blame: Essays in Cultural Theory*, Routledge, London.

Eisner H and J Leger (1988), "International Safety Rating System in South African Mining", *Journal of Occupational Accidents* (now *Safety Science*), vol 10, pp 141-160.

Engel G (1981), "The need for a new medical model: a challenge for biomedicine", Ch 5.7, in A Caplan, H Engelhardt and J McCartney (eds), *Concepts of Health and Disease: Interdisciplinary Perspectives*, Addison-Wesley, Reading, pp 589-607.

Esso Norway Team (2004), "The green and red roadmap to a safety culture where nobody gets hurt", paper delivered to the Society of Petroleum Engineers International Conference, Calgary.

Fischer D (nd), "Dependently sufficient causes in tort law - a reply to Professor Wright", unpublished paper, University of Missouri-Columbia.

Fitzpatrick J (1974), "Underground Mining: A Case Study of an Occupational Subculture of Danger", PhD thesis (S301.06/2).

Flüeler T and H Seiler (2003), "Risk-based regulation of technical risks: lessons learnt from case studies in Switzerland", *Journal of Risk Research*, vol 6, no 3, pp 213-231.

Garfinkel H (1967), *Studies in Ethnomethodology*, Prentice-Hall, Englewood Cliffs.

Gleick J (1998), *Chaos, The Amazing Science of the Unpredictable*, Vintage, London.

Gouldner A (1954), *Patterns of Industrial Bureaucracy*, Free Press, New York.

Hale A (2000), "Culture's confusions", *Safety Science*, vol 34, no 1, pp 1-14.

Hale A, T Heijer and F Koornneef (2003), "Management of safety rules: The case of railways", *Safety Science Monitor*, vol 7, no 1, pp 1-11.

Hall J (1994), "Review of Beck's Risk Society", *Sociological Review*, vol 42, pp 344-346.

Hawke A (2000), "People Power", accessed 17 November 2000, available at defweb6.cbr.defence.gov.au/secretary/.

Higson D (1989), *Risks to Individuals in NSW and in Australia as a Whole*, Australian Nuclear Science and Technology Organisation, Lucas Heights.

Hopkins A (1999), *Managing Major Hazards: The Lessons of the Moura Mine Disaster*, Allen & Unwin, Sydney.

Hopkins A (2000a), *Lessons from Longford*, CCH, Sydney.

Hopkins A (2000b), "A culture of denial: sociological similarities between the Moura and Gretley mine disasters", *Journal of Occupational Health and Safety — Australia and New Zealand*, vol 16, no 1, pp 29-36.

Hopkins A (2002), *Lessons from Longford: The Trial*, CCH, Sydney.

Horlick-Jones T (1995), "Modern disasters as outrage and betrayal", *International Journal of Mass Emergencies and Disasters*, November, vol 13, no 3, pp 305-315.

HSE (Health and Safety Executive) (2001), *Reducing Risks, Protecting People, HSE's Decision Making Process*, HMSO, Norwich.

Hudson P (nd), "Safety culture — the way ahead? Theory and practical principles", unpublished paper.

Hudson P (2003), Paper presented at the Aviation Psychology Conference, Sydney.

Janis I (1972), *Victims of Groupthink: A Psychological Study of Foreign Policy Decisions and Fiascos*, Houghton Mifflin, Boston.

Johnstone R (1997), *Occupational Health and Safety Law and Policy*, Law Book Company, Sydney.

JSTFADT (Joint Standing Committee on Foreign Affairs, Defence and Trade) (2001), *Rough Justice? An Investigation into Allegations of Brutality in the Army's Parachute Battalion*, Parliament of Australia, Canberra.

Kahn A (1984), *Social Psychology*, Brown, Dubuque.

LaPorte T and P Consolini (1991), "Working in practice but not in theory: the theoretical challenges of 'high-reliability organisations'", *Journal of Public Administration Research and Theory*, vol 1, no 1, pp 19-47.

Lawton R (1998), "Not working to rule: understanding procedural violations at work", *Safety Science*, vol 28, no 2, pp 77-95.

Leivesley S (2000), "The Adequacy of the Risk Management Procedures Applicable to the Circumstances of the Railway Accident at Glenbrook", unpublished report, July, p 3.

Leplat J (1998), "About implementation of safety rules", Safety Science, vol 29, pp 189-204.

Lupton D (1999), *Risk*, Routledge, London.

Marples D (1988), *The Social Impact of the Chernobyl Disaster*, St Martin's Press, New York.

McInerney P (2000a), *Interim Report of the Special Commission of Inquiry into the Glenbrook Rail Accident*, The Commission, Sydney.

McInerney P (2000b), *Second Interim Report of the Special Commission of Inquiry into the Glenbrook Rail Accident*, The Commission, Sydney.

McInerney P (2001), *Final Report of the Special Commission of Inquiry into the Glenbrook Rail Accident*, The Commission, Sydney.

NRCET (National Research Centre for Environmental Toxicology and Queensland Health Scientific Services) (2002), *Examination of the potential exposure of RAN personnel to polychlorinated dibenzodioxins and polychlorinated dibenzofurans, via drinking water, A report to the Department of Veterans Affairs*, available at www.dva.gov.au/DVA_NRCET_Final%20Reports.pdf.

Perrow C (1999), *Normal Accidents*, Princeton University Press, Princeton.

Pidgeon N, C Hood, D Jones, B Turner and R Gibson (1992), "Risk perception", Ch 5, in *Risk analysis, Perception and Management: Report of a Royal Society Study Group*, The Royal Society, London, pp 89-134.

Pitzer C (1999), *Safety Culture Survey Report: Australian Minerals Industry*, Minerals Council of Australia & SAFEmap, Canberra.

Pybus R (1996), *Safety Management: Strategy and Practice*, Butterworth Heinemann, Oxford.

R2A (Risk and Reliability Associates) (2002), *Risk and Reliability: An Introductory Text*, 4th ed, R2A, Melbourne.

Railtrack (1999), "Railway Safety Case", vol 1, unpublished document.

Rasmussen J (1997), "Risk management in a dynamic society: a modelling problem", *Safety Science*, vol 27, no 2/3, pp 183-213.

Reason J (1997), *Managing the Risks of Organisational Accidents*, Ashgate, Aldershot.

Reason J (2000), "Beyond the limitations of safety systems", *Australian Safety News*, April.

Roberts H (1993), "Review of Beck's Risk Society", *Sociology*, vol 27, pp 708-709.

Schein E (1992), *Organisational Culture and Leadership*, 2nd ed, Jossey-Bass, San Francisco.

Scott A (2000), "Risk Society or Angst Society?", Ch 2, in B Adam, U Beck and J Van Loon (eds), *The Risk Society and Beyond*, Sage, London, pp 33-46.

Shaw A and V Blewitt (2000), "What works? The strategies which help to integrate OHS management within business development and the role of the outsider", Ch 21, in K Frick, P Jensen, M Quinlan, and T Wilthagen (eds), *Systematic Occupational Health and Safety Management*, Pergamon, Amsterdam, pp 457-473.

Simard M and A Marchand (1997), "Workgroups' propensity to comply with safety rules: the influence of micro-macro organisational factors", *Ergonomics*, vol 40, no 2, pp 172-188.

Stephan S (2001), "Decision making in incident control teams", *Journal of Occupational Health and Safety — Australia and New Zealand*, vol 17, no 2, pp 135-145.

Tengs T, M Adams, D Safrau, J Siegel, M Weinstein and J Graham (1995), "Five-hundred life-saving interventions and their cost-effectiveness", *Risk Analysis*, vol 13, no 3, pp 369-390.

Thomas R (2000), "Getting the safety message", *OHS Alert*, vol 1, no 7, CCH, Sydney.

Turner B (1995), *Medical Power and Social Knowledge*, Sage, London.

Truss L (2003), *Eats, Shoots and Leaves: The Zero Tolerance Approach to Punctuation*, Profile, London.

Tweeddale M (2003), *Managing Risk and Reliability of Process Plants*, Gulf, Boston.

Uff J (2000), *The Southall Rail Accident Inquiry Report*, HSE, Norwich.

Uff J and L Cullen (2001), *The Southall and Ladbroke Grove Joint Inquiry into Train Protection Systems*, HSE Books, London.

Vaughan D (1996), *The Challenger Launch Decision*, University of Chicago Press, London.

Vatn J (1998), "A discussion of the acceptable risk problem", *Reliability Engineering and System Safety*, vol 61, no 1-2, pp 11-19.

Viner D (2002), "Risk assessments — do they work?", *Safety in Australia*, December, vol 24, no 3, pp 12-16.

VWA (Victorian WorkCover Authority), Major Hazard Division (2001), *Safety Management Systems under the Occupational Health and Safety (Major Hazard Facilities) Regulations*, MHD GN-12, September, available at www.workcover.vic.gov.au/vwa/home.nsf/pages/so_majhaz_guidance.

Weick K, K Sutcliffe and D Obstfeld (1999), "Organising for high reliability: processes of collective mindfulness", *Research in Organisational Behaviour*, vol 21, pp 81-123.

Weick K and K Sutcliffe (2001), *Managing the Unexpected: Assuring High Performance in an Age of Complexity*, Jossey-Bass, San Francisco.

Wells C (1993), *Corporations and Criminal Responsibility*, Clarendon, Oxford.

Yates A (2000), *Government as an Informed Buyer: Recognising Technical Expertise as a Crucial Factor in the Success of Engineering Contracts*, The Institution of Engineers Australia, Canberra.

Index

Page

Reports
   Glenbrook rail crash inquiry....... 26; 29; 66; 78
   Ladbroke Grove accident.............................44
   Southall rail crash (UK)................................33

Reprisals, fear of — see **Punishment**

Research, accident — see **Accident analysis**

Resilience
   commitment to.. 15

Responsibility — see **Culture of blame**

Risk assessment, quantitative —
   see **Quantitative risk assessment**

Risk aversion......................................146

Risk compensation theory.............................115

Risk exposure — see **Acceptable risk; Risk
   reduction**

Risk reduction
   cost effectiveness.................................. 126; 127
   reduction of exposure..........................132; 133

Risk society
   concept...139
   explanation of risk selection........................ 142
   increasing tendency to blame..............143–145
   interpretation...140
   objections...139; 140
   outrage and betrayal............................145; 146
   risks selected...141

Risk-awareness.......................................3
   augmentation of workplace safety
     rules...16; 17
   commitment of management........................ 18
   Glenbrook rail crash
   – commercial emphasis undermining
     infrastructure reliability............................. 63
   – disempowering of workforce...............73–75
   – effects of disaggregation....................... 62–64
   – impact of rules...38, 39

Page

   – isolation of signallers.......................45; 46; 74
   – lack of good accident investigation and
     risk reporting...................................70; 71; 73
   – lack of awareness throughout
     organisation......................... 61; 62; 71; 72; 74
   – need for fundamental change.................. 78
   – other examples of failure...................... 66; 67
   – over-emphasis on on time
     running..55; 59; 74
   – over-reliance on rules deadening
     awareness...................................39; 40; 67; 74
   – risk-blind or risk-denying....................61; 62
   – static hazard list...63
   – suggestions for fostering risk-focused
     approach..69; 70
   – suggestions for "golden rules"................. 68
   – unsatisfactory communications
     systems.. 64; 65
   incorporation into safety rules..................... 18
   promotion throughout
     organisation.. 18; 19
   RAAF priorities... 106

Risk-blind culture — see **Risk-awareness**

Risk-denial cultures..19
   ad hoc criteria.. 21
   downgrading intermittent warnings........... 21
   Glenbrook rail crash.............. 29; 42; 61; 66; 71
   groupthink.. 21; 22
   normalising the evidence...............................20
   onus of proof...21
   "we have it under control"...........................20

Risk-management approach
   rail track workers.. 69

Risk-reporting systems............................... 12; 70

Road accident fatality rates........................... 143
   United Kingdom.................................... 115; 128

Royal Australian Air Force — see **RAAF case
   study**

Rule 245
   Glenbrook rail crash..... 31; 34–36; 55; 147–150